WORDS
FOR A FINAL GENERATION

By David Hocking

WORDS for a Final Generation

Copyright 2016 by HFT Publications
PO Box 3927 Tustin, CA 92781
1-800-75-BIBLE

Printed in the United States of America

Unless noted otherwise, all Scripture is taken from The Holy Bible, King James Version, copyright 1982, by Thomas Nelson, Inc. Used by permission.

All rights reserved. No part of this publication may be reproduced, stored in a retrieval system, or transmitted in any form or by any means, electronic, mechanical, photocopying, recording, or otherwise, without the prior written consent of the Publisher.

ISBN : 978-0-939497-60-7

WORDS FOR A FINAL GENERATION

(Studies in Deuteronomy)

I Corinthians 10:11 – *"Now all these things happened unto them for examples, and they are written for our admonition, upon whom the ends of the world are come."*

INTRODUCTION

The name of the book, the 5th book of the Pentateuch (Law of Moses) is not *"Deuteronomy"* (which means "the second law"), but the original Hebrew name is *"Devarim"* which means *"WORDS"* – a plural form of the very common word *debar*.

Deuteronomy is quoted over 80 times in the New Testament, and appears to be the favorite book of our Lord Yeshua. Israel was commanded to read publicly the entire book at the annual Feast of Succoth (Tabernacles) at the end of the sabbatical year.

Deuteronomy 31:9-13 – *"And Moses wrote this law, and delivered it unto the priests, the sons Levi, who bore the ark of the covenant of the LORD, and unto all the elders of Israel. And Moses commanded them, saying, At the end of every seven years, in the solemnity of the year of release, in the feast of tabernacles, when all Israel is come to appear before the LORD thy God in the place which He shall choose, thou shalt read this law before all Israel in their hearing. Gather the people together, men, and women, and children, and thy stranger who is within thy gates, that they may hear, and that they may learn, and fear the LORD your God, and observe to do all the words of this law; And that their children, who have not known anything, may hear, and learn to fear the LORD your God, as long as ye live in the land to which ye go over the Jorden to possess it."*

The Jewish Publication Society in its amazing commentary on

Deuteronomy (*Sefer Devarim*) states the following on page 28:

"It would be difficult to overstate the extent of Deuteronomy's impact on Jewish life. No idea has done more to shape Jewish history than monotheism, which Deuteronomy asserts so passionately. And no verse had done more to shape Jewish consciousness and identity than the one that Judaism chose as the classic expression of the monotheistic idea, the SHEMA (Deuteronomy 6:4-5):

"Hear, O Israel: The LORD our God is one LORD; and thou shalt love the LORD thy God with all thine heart, and with all thy soul, and with all thy might."

GENERAL OUTLINE

DETAILS	PAGE
Introduction	4
General Outline	7
The Beginning (1:1-5)	12

DISCOURSE #1

God's <u>CALL</u> (1:6-2:23)	15
The <u>CONFLICT</u> with Sihon (2:24-37)	27
The <u>CONQUEST</u> of OG (3:1-11)	31
The <u>CONTROL</u> of Land (East) (3:12-17)	33
The <u>COMMITMENT</u> to help (3:18-20)	35
The <u>COMMAND</u> to Joshua (3:21-29)	36
The <u>COMMANDS</u> of the LORD (4:1-49)	39

The **COMMANDMENTS** for God's people (5:1-33)	55
The **CHALLENGE** of the LORD (6:1-25)	67
The **CHOOSING** of Israel as the people of God (7:1-26)	78
The **CAUTION** of the LORD (8:1-20)	87
The **CLEANSING** of His people (9:1-29)	97
The **CIRCUMCISION** of the heart (10:1-22)	108
The **CARE** of the Land (11:1-32)	117

DISCOURSE #2

The **CHOICE** of the places from the LORD! (12:1-32)	129

The <u>CONFUSION</u> about false prophets (13:1-18)	139
The <u>CHARACTER</u> of their holiness (14:1-29)	148
The <u>CONCERN</u> for the poor (15:1-23)	158
The <u>CELEBRATIONS</u> of Jewish worship (16:1-22)	170
The <u>CARFULNESS</u> needed in offering sacrifices (17:1-20)	179
The <u>COMING</u> of a prophet (18:1-22)	190
The <u>CITIES</u> of judgment (19:1-21)	196
The <u>CONFLICTS</u> that lead to war (20:1-20)	205
The <u>CONQUEST</u> of pagan cultures (21:1-23)	214

The **CONCERNS** of relationships (22:1-30)	225
The **CALL** and **CLEANSING** for worship (23:1-25)	236
The **CONSIDERATION** of marriage & money matters (24:1-22)	243
The **CONTROVERSIES** that must be resolved (25:1-19)	252
The **CARRYING** of the First Fruits to God	259

DISCOURSE #3

The **CURSES** to be remembered (27:1-26)	269
The **CAUSES** behind the curses (28:1-68)	277

The **CONSEQUENCES** of of blessings and curses (29:1-29)	296
The **CALL** to repentance (30:1-20)	304
The **COURAGE** which Moses declared they would need (31:1-30)	310
The **COMPLETION** of the Song of Moses and the dangers (32:1-52)	325
The **COMING** of blessing upon the people (33:1-29)	342
The **CONCLUSION** of the life of Moses (34:1-12)	354

THE BEGINNING

Deuteronomy 1:1-5

"These are the words which Moses spoke unto all Israel on this side of the Jordan in the wilderness, in the Arabah ("plain" or "wilderness") *over against the Red Sea, between Paran, and Tophel, and Laban, and Hazeroth, and Dizahab. (It is eleven days' journey from Horeb by the way of Mount Seir unto Kadesh-barnea.) And it came to pass in the fortieth year, in the eleventh month, on the first day of the month, that Moses spoke unto the children of Israel, according unto all that the LORD had given him in commandment unto them, After he had slain Sihon, the king of the Amorites, who dwelt in Heshbon, and Og, the king of Bashan, who dwelt in Astaroth in Edrei, On this*

side of the Jordan, in the land of Moab, began Moses to declare this law, saying,"

1. The <u>PROCLAMATION</u> – *"These are the words which Moses spake"*

2. The <u>PEOPLE</u> to whom this proclamation was given – *"unto all Israel"*

3. The <u>PLACE</u> where these words were spoken – *"on this side Jordan in the wilderness, in the plain over against the Red Sea, between Paran, and Tophel, and Laban, and Hazeroth, and Dizahab."*

4. The <u>PROPHET</u> whom God used to speak to His people!

Deuteronomy 34:10-12 – *"And there arose not a prophet since in Israel like unto Moses, whom the*

LORD knew face to face, in all the signs and the wonders which the LORD send him to do in the land of Egypt to Pharaoh, and to all his servants, and to all his land, And in all that mighty hand, and in all the great terror which Moses showed in the sight of all Israel."

5. The <u>POINT</u> in time when these words were given!

"the 40th year, in the 11th month, on the first day of the month...after he had slain Sihon...and Og...in the land of Moab"

THE CALL OF GOD
Deuteronomy 1:6–2:23

1. To <u>DEPART</u> from Mount Horeb – 1:6-8

"The LORD our God spoke unto us in Horeb, saying, Ye have dwelt long enough in this mount; Turn you, and take your journey, and go to the mount of the Amorites, and unto all the places nigh thereto, in the Arabah, in the hills, and in the Shephelah, and in the Negev, by the seaside, to the land of the Canaanites, and unto Lebanon, unto the great river, the river Euphrates. Behold, I have set the land before you; go in and possess the land which the LORD swore unto your fathers, Abraham, Isaac, and Jacob, to give unto them and to their seed after them."

2. To <u>DESIGNATE</u> wise leaders to help Moses – 1:9-18

   (1) The <u>INABILITY</u> of Moses to handle all the problems – 1:9-12

"And I spoke unto you at that time, saying, I am not able to bear you myself alone. The LORD your God hath multiplied you and, behold, ye are this day as the stars of heaven for multitude. (The LORD God of your fathers make you a thousand times as many more as ye are, and bless you, as He hath promised you!) How can I myself alone bear your weight, and your burden, and your strife?"

   (2) The <u>INVITATION</u> to wise men – 1:13-15

"Take you wise men, and understanding, and known

among your tribes, and I will make them rulers over you. And ye answered me, and said, The thing which thou hast spoken is good for us to do. So I took the chief of your tribes, wise men, and known, and made them heads over you, captains over thousands, and captains over hundreds, and captains over fifties, and captains over tens, and officers among your tribes."

> (3) The <u>INSTRUCTION</u> that Moses gave to these leaders – 1:16-18

"And I charged your judges at that time, saying, Hear the causes between your brethren, and judge righteously between every man and his brother, and the stranger who is with him. Ye shall not respect persons in judgment, but ye shall hear the small as well as

the great; ye shall not be afraid of the face of man, for the judgment is God's; and the cause that is too hard for you, bring it unto me, and I will hear it. And I commanded you at that time all the things which ye should do."

 3. To <u>DEFEAT</u> the Amorites – 1:19-46

  (1) The <u>CONDITION</u> of their travels – 1:19

"And when we departed from Horeb, we went through all that great and terrible wilderness, which ye saw by the way of the mountain of the Amorites, as the LORD our God commanded us; and we came to Kadesh-barnea."

  (2) The <u>CHALLENGE</u> concerning the Amorites – 1:20-21

"And I said unto you, Ye are come unto the mountain of the Amorites, which the LORD our God doth give unto us. Behold, the LORD thy God hath set the land before thee. Go up and possess it, as the LORD God of thy fathers hath said unto thee; fear not, neither be discouraged."

    (3)   The <u>CHOOSING</u> of 12 men to spy out the Land – vv. 22-25

"And ye came near unto me, every one of you, and said, We will send men before us, and they shall search out the land, and bring us word again by what way we must go up, and into what cities we shall come. And the saying pleased me well; and I took twelve men of you, one of a tribe. And they turned and went up into the mountain, and came unto the

valley of Eshcol, and searched it out. And they took of the fruit of the land in their hands, and brought it down unto us, and brought us word again, and said, It is a good land which the LORD our God doth give us."

      (4)   The <u>CONCERN</u> of the people – vv. 26-28

"Notwithstanding ye would not go up, but rebelled against the commandment of the LORD your God; And ye murmured in your tents, and said, Because the LORD hated us, He hath bought us forth out of the land of Egypt, to deliver us into the hand of the Amorites, to destroy us. Where shall we go up? Our brethren have discouraged our heart, saying, The people are greater and taller than we; the cities are great and walled up to heaven; and,

moreover, we have seen the sons of the Anakim there."

    (5)   The <u>COMFORT</u> of the LORD – vv. 29-31

"Then I said unto them, Dread not, neither be afraid of them. The LORD your God, Who goeth before you, He shall fight for you, according to all that He did for you in Egypt before your eyes; And in the wilderness, where thou hast seen how that the LORD thy God bore thee, as a man doth bear his son, in all the way that ye went, until ye came into this place."

The LORD's comfort involved two primary issues: One, His presence, and two, His promise – *"He shall fight for you."*

    (6)   The <u>COLLAPSE</u> of their confidence – vv. 32-33

"Yet in this thing ye did not believe the LORD your God. Who went in the way before you, to search you out a place to pitch your tents in, in fire by night, to show you by what way ye should go, and in a cloud by day."

    (7)   The <u>CONSEQUENCE</u> of their rebellion – vv. 34-40

"And the LORD heard the voice of your words, and was wroth, and swore, saying, Surely there shall not one of these men of this evil generation see that good land, which I swore to give unto your fathers, save Caleb, the son of Jephunneh; he shall see it, and to him will I give the land that he hath trodden upon, and to his children, because he hath wholly followed the LORD. Also the LORD was angry with me for your

sakes, saying, Thou also shalt not go in there. But Joshua, the son of Nun, who standeth before thee, he shall go in there: encourage him; for he shall cause Israel to inherit it. Moreover your little ones, who ye said should be a prey, and your children, who in that day had no knowledge between good and evil, they shall go in there, and unto them will I give it, and they shall possess it. But as for you, turn you, and take your journey into the wilderness by the way of the Red Sea."

    (8)   The <u>CIRCUMSTANCE</u> which led to their defeat by the Amorites – vv. 41-46

"Then ye answered and said unto Me, We have sinned against the LORD; we will go up and fight, according to all that the LORD

our God commanded us. And when ye had girded on every man his weapon of war, ye were ready to go up into the hill. And the LORD said unto me, Say unto them, Go not up, neither fight, for I am not among you; lest ye be smitten before your enemies. So I spoke unto you; and ye would not hear, but rebelled against the commandment of the LORD, and went presumptuously up into the hill. And the Amorites, who dwelt in that mountain, came out against you, and chased you as bees do, and destroyed you in Seir, even unto Hormah. And ye returned and wept before the LORD; but the LORD would not hearken to your voice, nor give ear unto you. So ye abode in Kadesh many days, according unto the days that ye abode there."

4. To **DISTRESS** not Edom, Moab, or Ammon – 2:1-23

    (1) The **COMMAND** to stop wandering and go north – vv. 1-7

    (2) The **CAUTION** about fighting the Moabites – vv. 8-18

"Distress not the Moabites, neither contend with them in their land for a possession.

In Deuteronomy 2:10-12 we have a reminder of the *"giants"* (Emims) – *"a people great, and many, and tall, as the Anakims* (Numbers 13:33) – *the children of Esau succeeded them…dwelt in their stead; as Israel did unto the land of his possession, which the LORD gave unto them"*

    (3) The **CONCERN** about the Ammonites – vv. 19-23

The REASON for not getting involved with them – v. 19 – *"for I will NOT give thee of the land of the children of Ammon any possession; because I have given it unto the children of Lot for a possession."*

The RESULT the LORD brought upon the giants – vv. 20-23

The LORD destroyed them before them – a people great and many, and tall, as the Anakims."

The <u>CONFLICT</u> with Sihon the Giant
Deuteronomy 2:24-37

1. The <u>PROMISE</u> of his land – v. 24

"Rise ye up, take your journey, and pass over the river Arnon; behold, I have given into thine hand Sihon, the Amorite King of Heshbon, and his land. Begin to possess it, and contend with him in battle."

2. The <u>PANIC</u> that God will cause – v. 25

"This day will I begin to put the dread of thee and the fear of thee upon the nations that are under the whole heaven, who shall hear report of thee, and shall tremble and be in anguish because of thee."

3, The <u>PROBLEM</u> which Sihon created – vv. 26-31

"And I sent messengers out of the wilderness of Kedemoth unto Sihon, King of Heshbon, with words of peace, saying, Let me pass through thy land; I will go along by the highway, I will neither turn unto the right hand not to the left. Thou shalt sell me meat for money, that I may eat; and give me water for money, that I may drink: only I will pass through on my feet (As the children of Esau who dwell in Seir, and the Moabites who dwell in Ar, did unto me) until I shall pass over the Jordan into the land which the LORD our God giveth us. But Sihon, King of Heshbon, would not let us pass by him; for the LORD thy God hardened his spirit, and made his heart obstinate, that He might deliver

him into thy hand, as appeareth this day. And the LORD said unto me, Behold, I have begun to give Sihon and his land before thee; begin to possess it, that thou mayest inherit his land."

    4. The <u>POWER</u> of God was displayed – vv. 32-37

"Then Sihon came out against us, he and all his people, to fight at Jahaz. And the LORD our God delivered him before us, and we smote him, and his sons, and all his people. And we took all his cities at that time, and utterly destroyed the men, and the women, and the little ones of every city; we left none to remain. Only the cattle we took for a prey unto ourselves, and the spoil of the cities which we took. From Aroer, which is by the brink of the river of Arnon, and from the city

that is by the river, even unto Gilead, there was not one city too strong for us; the LORD our God delivered all unto us. Only unto the land of the children of Ammon thou camest not, nor unto any place of the river Jabbok, nor unto the cities in the mountains, nor unto whatsoever the LORD our God forbade us."

The deliverance came from the LORD, and the destruction was awesome – *"we left none to remain."*

The <u>CONQUEST</u> of Og, the last of the giants
Deuteronomy 3:1-11

"Then we turned, and went up the way to Bashan, and Og, the King of Bashan, came out against us, he and all his people, to battle at Edrei. And the LORD said unto me, Fear him not; for I will deliver him, and all his people, and his land, into thy hand, and thou shalt do unto him as thou didst unto Sihon, King of the Amorites, who dwelt at Heshbon. So the LORD our God delivered into our hands Og also the king of Bashan, and all his people, and we smote him until none was left to him remaining. And we took all his cities at that time; there was not a city which we took not from them, threescore cities, all the region of Argob, the kingdom of Og in

Bashan. All these cities were fenced with high walls, gates, and bars, beside unwalled towns, a great many. And we utterly destroyed them, as we did unto Sihon, King of Heshbon, utterly destroying the men, women, and children of every city. But all the cattle and the spoil of the cities, we took for a prey to ourselves. And we took at that time, out of the hand of the two kings of the Amorites, the land that was on this side of the Jordan, from the river of Arnon unto Mount Hermon. (which Hermon the Sidonians call Sirion; and the Amorites call it Senir); All the cities of the plain, and all Gilead, and all Bashan, unto Salecah and Edrei, cities of the kingdom of Og in Bashan. For only Og, King of Bashan, remained of the remnant of giants; behold, his bedstead *was a bedstead of iron. Is it not in Rabbah of the children of Ammon? Nine cubits was the length thereof, and four cubits the breadth of it, after the cubit of a man."*

The <u>CONTROL</u> of the land east of Jordan
Deuteronomy 3:12-17

"And this land, which we possessed at that time, from Aroer, which is by the river Arnon, and half of Mount Gilead, and the cities thereof, gave I unto the Reubenites and to the Gadites. And the rest of Gilead, and all Bashan, being the kingdom of Og, gave I unto the half tribe of Manasseh; all the region of Argob, with all Bashan, which was called the land of giants. Jair, the son of Manasseh took all the country of

Argob unto the coasts of the Geshurites and the Maachathites, even Bashan, and called them after his own name, Havvothjair, unto this day. And I gave Gilead unto Machir. And unto the Reubenites and unto the Gadites I gave from Gilead, even unto the river Arnon, half the valley, and the border even unto the river Jabbok, which is the border of the children of Ammon; The plain also, and the Jordan, and the coast thereof, from Chinnereth even unto the sea of the plain, even the Salt Sea, under Ashdoth-pisgah eastward."

The dimensions and the description of this land was best summarized as *"all Bashan, which was called the land of giants."*

The <u>COMMITMENT</u> of these tribes to help in the conquests west of the Jordan River –
vv. 18-20

"And I commanded you at that time, saying, The LORD your God hath given you this land to possess it; ye shall pass over armed before your brethren, the children of Israel, all who are meet for the war. But your wives, and your little ones, and your cattle (for I know that ye have much cattle) shall abide in your cities which I have given you, Until the LORD have given rest unto your brethren, as well as unto you, and until they also possess the land which the LORD your God hath given them beyond the Jordan; and then shall ye

return every man unto his possession which I have given you."

1. The **POSSESSION** of the Land – v. 18 – *"all that are meet for the war"*

2. The **PROTECTION** of their families and possessions – v. 19 – *"abide in the cities which I have given you"*

3. The **PEACE** of the land – v. 20 – *"Until the LORD have given rest unto your brethren, as well as unto you"*

The **COMMAND** to Joshua by Moses
vv. 21-29

"And I commanded Joshua at that time, saying, Thine eyes have seen all that the LORD your God hath done unto these two kings; so

shall the LORD do unto all the kingdoms where thou passest. Ye shall not fear them; for the LORD your God shall fight for you. And I besought the LORD at that time, saying, O Lord GOD, Thou hast begun to show Thy servant Thy greatness, and Thy mighty hand, for what God is there in haven or in earth, Who can do according to Thy works, and according to Thy might? I pray thee, let me go over and see the good land that is beyond the Jordan, that goodly mountain, and Lebanon. But the LORD was wroth with me for your sakes, and would not hear me; and the LORD said unto me, Let it suffice thee; speak no more unto Me of this mater. Get thee up into the top of Pisgah, and lift up thine eyes westward, and northward, and southward, and eastward, and behold it with thine eyes; for thou shalt not go over this Jordan. But charge Joshua, and encourage him, and strengthen him; for he shall go over before this people, and he shall cause them to inherit the land which thou shalt see. So we abode in the valley over against Beth-peor."

1. The **RESPONSE** of the LORD – vv. 21-22 – *"for the LORD your God He shall fight for you."*

2. The **REQUEST** of Moses that was denied – vv. 23-27- *"let me go over and see the good land..."*

3. The **RESPONSIBILITY** Moses had toward Joshua – vv. 28-29 – *"charge Joshua, and encourage him, and strengthen him"*

THE **COMMANDS** OF THE LORD

Deuteronomy 4:1-49

1. The **PURPOSE** behind His commands – v. 1

"Now therefore hearken, O Israel, unto the statutes and unto the judgments, which I teach you, to do them, that ye may live, and go in and possess the land which the LORD God of your fathers giveth you."

2. The main **PREREQUISITE** of these commands – v. 2

"Ye shall not add unto the word which I command you, neither shall ye diminish ought from it, that ye may keep the commandments of the LORD your God which I command you."

Joshua 1:7-8 – *"Only be thou strong and very courageous, that thou mayest observe to do according to all the law, which Moses, My servant, commanded thee; turn not from it to the right hand or to the left, that thou mayest prosper wherever thou goest. This book of the law shall not depart out of thy mouth, but thou shalt meditate therein day and night, that thou mayest observe to do according to all that is written therein; for then thou shalt make thy way prosperous, and then thou shalt have good success."*

Proverbs 30:5-6 – *"Every word of God is pure; He is a Shield unto those who put their trust in Him. Add thou not unto His words, lest He reprove thee, and thou be found a liar."*

3. The <u>PROSPERITY</u> that will come – vv. 3-4

"Your eyes have seen what the LORD did because of Baal-peor, for all the men who followed Baal-peor, the LORD thy God hath destroyed them from among you. But ye who did cleave unto the LORD your God are alive, every one of you this day."

What a blessing to see the way God prospered His people for one big reason – *"ye who did cleave unto the LORD your God."*

4. The <u>PROMISE</u> of wisdom and understanding – vv. 5-8

"Behold, I have taught you statutes and judgments, even as the LORD my God commanded me, that ye should do so in the land to which ye go to possess it. Keep, therefore, and do them; for

this is your wisdom and your understanding in the sight of the nations, who shall hear all these statutes and say, Surely this great nation is a wise and understanding people. For what nation is there so great, who hath God as nigh unto them, as the LORD our God is in all things that we call upon Him for? And what nation is there so great, that hath statutes and judgments as righteous as all this law, which I set before you this day?"

1. **It includes the <u>NEARNESS</u> of the LORD** – *"For what nation is there so great, who hath God as nigh unto them, as the LORD our God is in all things that we call upon Him for"*

2. **It involves the <u>NATURE</u> of these commands** – *"as righteous as all this law"*

5. The **PRIORITY** which these commands should be in our lives – vv. 9-24

   (1) As to **FORGETTING** what you have seen and heard – v. 9

"Only take heed to thyself, and keep thy soul diligently, lest thou forget the things which thine eyes have seen, and lest they depart from thy heart all the days of thy life; but teach them to thy sons, and thy sons' sons"

   (2) As to **FEARING** the LORD – v. 10

"Specially the day that thou stoodest before the LORD thy God in Horeb, when the LORD said unto me, Gather me the people together, and I will make them hear My words, that they may learn to fear Me all the days that

they shall live upon the earth, and that they may teach their children."

  (3) As to <u>FOLLOWING</u> His covenant – v. 13

"And He declared unto you His covenant, which He commanded you to perform, even Ten Commandments; and He wrote them upon two tables of stone."

  (4) As to <u>FORSAKING</u> idolatry – vv. 16-19

"Lest ye corrupt yourselves, and make you a graven image, the similitude of any figure, the likeness of male or female, the likeness of any beast that is on the earth, the likeness of any winged fowl that flieth in the air, the likeness of anything that creepeth on the ground, the likeness of any fish that is in the waters beneath

the earth; And lest thou lift up thine eyes unto heaven, and when thou seest the sun, and the moon, and the stars, even all the host of heaven, shouldest be driven to worship them, and serve them, which the LORD thy God hath divided unto all nations under the whole heaven."

    (5)   As to <u>FACING</u> the anger of the LORD – vv. 20-24

"But the LORD hath taken you, and brought you forth out of the iron furnace, even out of Egypt, to be unto him a people of inheritance, as ye are this day. Furthermore, the LORD was angry with me for your sakes, and swore that I should not go over the Jordan, and that I should not go in unto that good land, which the LORD thy God giveth thee for an inheritance; But I must die in

this land. I must not go over the Jordan. But ye shall go over, and possess that good land. Take heed unto yourselves, lest ye forget the covenant of the LORD your God, which He made with you, and make you a graven image, or the likeness of anything, which the LORD thy God hath forbidden thee. For the LORD thy God is a consuming fire, even a jealous God."

The **DELIVERANCE** from Egypt must never be forgotten, as well as the **DISOBEDIENCE** of Moses, and we certainly must always remember that the **DISPLAY** of God's nature involves His jealousy and anger – He is a *"consuming fire."*

    6. The **PUNISHMENT** for following idolatry – vv. 25-28

"When thou shalt beget children, and children's children, and ye shall have remained long in the land, and shall corrupt yourselves, and make a graven image, or the likeness of anything, and shall do evil in the sight of the LORD thy God, to provoke Him to anger, I call heaven and earth to witness against you this day, that ye shall soon utterly perish from off the land whereunto ye go over the Jordan to possess it; ye shall not prolong your days upon it, but shall utterly be destroyed. And the LORD shall scatter you among the nations, and ye shall be left few in number among the heathen, where the LORD shall lead you. And there ye shall serve gods, the work of men's hands, wood and stone, which neither see, nor hear, nor eat, nor smell."

(1) It <u>PROVOKES</u> God to anger – v. 25 – *"shall do evil in the sight of the LORD thy God, to provoke Him to anger."*

(2) It <u>PREDICTS</u> utter destruction – v. 26 – *"Ye shall soon utterly perish from off the land…"*

(3) It <u>PUTS</u> His people in heathen lands – vv. 27-29 – *"the LORD shall scatter you among the nations"*

7. The <u>POSSIBILITY</u> of forgiveness – vv. 29-40

(1) SEEK the LORD with all your heart and soul! v. 29

"But if from there thou shalt seek the LORD thy God, thou shalt find Him, if thou seek Him with all thy heart and with all thy soul."

(2) <u>SUBMIT</u> to His voice in times of tribulation! – v. 30

"When thou art in tribulation, and all these things are come upon thee, even in the latter days, if thou turn to the LORD thy God, and shalt be obedient unto His voice..."

(3) <u>SEARCH</u> for any evidence of the mercy of God! vv. 31-34

"(For the LORD thy God is a merciful God), He will not forsake thee, neither destroy thee, nor forget the covenant of thy fathers which He swore unto them. For ask now of the days that are past, which were before thee, since the day that God created man upon the earth, and ask from the one side of heaven unto the other,

whether there hath been any such thing as this great thing is, or hath been heard like it? Did ever people hear the voice of God speaking out of the midst of the fire, as thou hast heard, and live? Or hath God assayed to go and take him a nation from the midst of another nation, by temptations, by signs, and by wonders, and by war, and by a mighty hand, and by an outstretched arm, and by great terrors, according to all that the LORD your God did for you in Egypt before your eyes?"

THREE POWERFUL THINGS FROM THE LORD GOD OF ISRAEL:

He will not forsake thee!

He will not destroy thee!

He will not forget His covenant!

(4) **<u>SURRENDER</u>** to His power and plan! vv. 35-40

"Unto thee it was shown, that thou mightest know that the LORD, He is God; there is none else beside Him. Out of heaven He made thee to hear His voice, that He might instruct thee; and upon earth He showed thee His great fire, and thou heardest His words out of the midst of the fire. And because He loved thy father, therefore He chose their seed after them, and brought thee out in His sight with His mighty power out of Egypt, To drive out nations from before thee greater and mightier than thou art, to bring thee in, to give thee their land for an inheritance, as it is this day. Know therefore this day, and consider it in thine heart, that the LORD, He is God in heaven above,

and upon the earth beneath; there is none else. Thou shalt keep, therefore, His statutes, and His commandments, which I command thee this day, that it may go well with thee, and with thy children after thee, and that thou mayest prolong thy days upon the earth, which the LORD thy God giveth thee, forever."

    8. The <u>PLACING</u> of cities of refuge on the east side of the Jordan River – vv. 41-43

"Then Moses severed three cities on this side of the Jordan toward the sunrising. That the slayer might flee there, who should kill his neighbor unawares, and hated him not in times past, and that, fleeing unto one of these cities he might live. Namely, Bezer in the wilderness, in the plain country, of the Reubenites; and Ramoth in

Gilead, of the Gadites; and Golan in Bashan, of the Manassites."

   9. The **POSSESSION** of the land east of the Jordan River – vv. 44-49

"And this is the law which Moses set before the children of Israel; These are the testimonies, and the statutes, and the judgments, which Moses spoke unto the children of Israel, after they came forth out of Egypt, On this side of the Jordan, in the valley over against Beth-peor, in the land of Sihon, King of the Amorites, who dwelt at Heshbon, whom Moses and the children of Israel smote, after they were come forth out of Egypt. And they possessed his land, and the land of Og, King of Bashan, two kings of the Amorites who were on this side of the Jordan toward the sunrising;

From Aroer, which is by the bank of the river Arnon, even unto Mount Sion, which is Hermon, And all the plain on this side of the Jordan eastward, even unto the sea of the plain, under the springs of Pisgah."

The **COMMANDMENTS** for God's people
Deuteronomy 5:1-33

1. The **REMINDER** of what happened in Horeb – vv. 1-5

"And Moses called all Israel, and said unto them, Hear, O Israel, the statutes and judgments which I speak in your ears this day, that ye may learn them, and keep, and do them. The LORD our God made a covenant with us in Horeb. The LORD made not this covenant with our fathers, but with us, even us, who are all of us here alive this day. The LORD talked with you face to face in the mount out of the midst of the fire (I stood between the LORD and you at that time, to show you the word of the LORD; for ye were afraid by reason of the

fire, and went not up into the mount), saying"

    (1)   The <u>PURPOSE</u> behind the statutes and judgments

"that ye may learn them, and keep, and do them."

    (2)   The <u>PERSON</u> who gave the covenant

"The LORD our God made a covenant with us"

    (3)   The <u>PEOPLE</u> who were given this covenant

"with us, even us, who are all of us here alive this day"

    (4)   The <u>PRESENCE</u> of the LORD was heard and seen

"The LORD talked with you face to face in the mount out of the midst of the fire"

    2. The <u>REPETITION</u> of the LORD's commands – vv. 6-21

        (1)   NO OTHER GODS – v. 7

"Thou shalt have no other gods before Me"

        (2)   NO GRAVEN IMAGES – VV. 8-10

"Thou shalt not make thee any graven image, or any likeness of anything that is in heaven above, or that is in the earth beneath, or that is in the waters beneath the earth. Thou shalt not bow down thyself unto them, nor serve them; for I the LORD thy God am a jealous God, visiting the iniquity of the fathers upon the children unto the third and fourth

generation of them who hate Me, and showing mercy unto thousands of them who love Me and keep My commandments."

(3) NO TAKING THE LORD'S NAME IN VAIN! v. 11

"Thou shalt not take the Name of the LORD thy God in vain; for the LORD will not hold him guiltless who taketh His Name in vain."

(4) HONOR THE SABBATH DAY! vv. 12-15

"Keep the Sabbath Day to sanctify it, as the LORD thy God hath commanded thee. Six days thou shalt labor, and do all thy work; But the seventh day is the Sabbath of the LORD thy God: in it thou shalt not do any work, thou, nor thy son, nor thy daughter, nor thy

manservant, nor thy maidservant, nor thine ox, nor thine ass, nor any of thy cattle, nor thy stranger who is within thy gates; that thy manservant and thy maidservant may rest as well as thou. And remember that thou wast a servant in the land of Egypt, and that the LORD thy God brought thee out from there through a mighty hand and by a stretched out arm; therefore the LORD thy God commanded thee to keep the Sabbath Day."

(5) HONOR YOUR FATHER AND MOTHER – v. 16

"Honor thy father and they mother, as the LORD thy God hath commanded thee, that thy days may be prolonged, and that it may go well with thee in the land

which the LORD thy God giveth thee."

    (6)   **DO NOT KILL – v. 17**

"Thou shalt not kill"

    (7)   **NEITHER SHALT THOU COMMIT ADULTERY – v. 18**

"Neither shalt thou commit adultery"

    (8)   **NEITHER SHALT THOU STEAL – v. 19**

" Neither shalt thou steal"

    (9)   **DO NOT BEAR FALSE WITNESS – v. 20**

" Neither shalt thou bear false witness against thy neighbor"

(10) DO NOT COVET – v. 21

"Neither shalt thou desire thy neighbor's wife, neither shalt thou covet thy neighbor's house, his field, or his manservant, or his maidservant, his ox, or his ass, or anything that is thy neighbor's."

Ephesians 5:3-5 – *"But fornication, and all uncleanness, or covetousness, let it not be once named among you, as becometh saints; Neither filthiness, nor foolish talking, nor jesting, which are not convenient; but, rather, giving of thanks. For this ye know, that no whoremonger, nor unclean person, nor covetous man (who is an idolater) hath any inheritance in the kingdom of Christ and of God."*

Colossians 3:5 – *"Mortify, therefore, your members which* *are upon the earth; fornication, uncleanness, inordinate affection, evil concupiscence, and covetousness (which is idolatry)."*

3. The <u>REVELATION</u> of His powerful voice – vv. 22-26

"These words the LORD spoke unto all your assembly in the mount out of the midst of the fire, of the cloud, and of the thick darkness, with a great voice; and He added no more. And He wrote them in two tables of stone, and delivered them unto me. And it came to pass, when ye heard the voice out of the midst of the darkness (for the mountain did burn with fire), that ye came near unto me, even all the heads of your tribes, and your elders. And ye said, Behold, the LORD our

God hath shown us His glory and His greatness, and we have heard His voice out of the midst of the fire; we have seen this day that God doth talk with man, and he liveth. Now, therefore, why should we die? For this great fire will consume us; if we hear the voice of the LORD our God anymore, then we shall die. For who is there of all flesh, who hath heard the voice of the living God speaking out of the midst of the fire, as we have, and lived?"

SPECIAL WORDS – "the LORD our God hath shown us His glory and His greatness"

The <u>RESPONSE</u> of the Lord Himself – vv. 27-33

"Go thou near, and hear all that the LORD our God shall say; and speak thou unto us all that the

LORD our God shall speak unto thee, and we will hear it, and do it. And the LORD heard the voice of your words, when ye spoke unto me; and the LORD said unto me, I have heard the voice of the words of this people, which they have spoken unto thee; they have well said all that they have spoken. Oh, that there were such an heart in them, that they would fear Me, and keep all My commandments always, that it might be well with them and with their children forever! Go say to them, Get you into your tents again. But as for thee, stand thou here by Me, and I will speak unto thee all the commandments, and the statutes, and the judgments, which thou shalt teach them, that they may do them in the land which I give them to possess. Ye shall observe to do, therefore, as the LORD your God hath commanded you; ye shall not turn aside, to the right hand or to the left. Ye shall walk in all the ways which the LORD your God hath commanded you, that ye may live, and that it may be well with you, and that ye may prolong your days in the land which ye shall possess."

1. The **PROMISE** they made to Moses – v. 27 – *"we will hear it, and do it"*

2. The **PLEASURE** of the LORD at what they said – v. 28 – *"they have well said all that they have spoken"*

3. The **PRIORITY** which the LORD placed on what they said – v. 29 – *"O that there were such an heart in them"*

4. The **PRINCIPLES** which must govern what they said – vv. 30-33

    (1) LEARNING – *"which thou shalt teach them"*

    (2) LOYALTY – *"ye shall not turn aside to the right hand or to the left"*

    (3) LIFESTYLE – *"Ye shall walk in all the ways which the LORD your God hath commanded you"*

The **CHALLENGE** of the LORD – Deuteronomy 6:1-25

1. **FEAR GOD!** We need a deep REVERENCE for God Himself!

v. 2 – *"that thou mightiest fear the LORD thy God"*

v. 13 – *"Thou shalt fear the LORD thy God"*

v. 24 – *"And the LORD commanded us to do all these statutes, to fear the LORD our God for our good always..."*

(1) It involves **PRIORITIES** that are God-centered!

Psalm 5:7 – *"But as for me, I will come into Thy house in the multitude of Thy mercy; and in*

Thy fear will I worship toward Thy holy temple."

Psalm 22:23 – *"Ye who fear the LORD, praise Him; all ye, the seed of Jacob, glorify Him; and fear Him, all ye, the seed of Israel."*

Psalm 115:11 – *"Ye that fear the LORD, trust in the LORD, He is their help and their shield."*

> (2) It includes the <u>PURSUIT</u> of wisdom and knowledge!

Proverbs 1:7 – *"The fear of the LORD is the beginning of knowledge"*

Proverbs 9:10 – *"The fear of the LORD is the beginning of wisdom, and the knowledge of the Holy One is understanding."*

(3) It gives **PROTECTION** against temptation and sin!

Proverbs 8:13 – *"The fear of the LORD is to hate evil; pride, and arrogance, and the evil way.."*

Proverbs 14:16 – *"A wise man feareth, and departeth from evil"*

Proverbs 16:6 – *"By mercy and truth iniquity is purged; and by the fear of the LORD men depart from evil."*

2. **OBEY GOD!** We need a clear **REALIZATION** of our accountability to God!

v. 2 – *"to keep all His statutes and His commandments which I command thee, thou, and thy son, and thy son's son, all the days of thy life..."*

vv. 17-18 – *"Ye shall diligently keep the commandments of the LORD your God, and His testimonies, and His statutes, which He had commanded thee."*

v. 25 – *"And it shall be our righteousness, if we observe to do all these commandments before the LORD our God, as He hath commanded us."*

3. <u>**WORSHIP GOD!**</u> We need a strong <u>**RELIANCE**</u> upon God's character!

The words of Deuteronomy 6:4-9 are inscribed on a small piece of parchment and placed inside the *mezuzah* (meaning "doorpost") which is placed on the door posts where you enter your house.

    (1)   It means you have a personal <u>COMMITMENT</u> to

God – *"the LORD our God"*

    (2) It means you have total <u>CONFIDENCE</u> that the LORD is the only God there is – *"one LORD"*

The Hebrew word for *"one"* can mean "more than one" – *echad* – The Hebrew word that means "one and only one" is the word *yachid*.

4. <u>LOVE GOD!</u> We need a loving <u>RELATIONSHIP</u> to God Himself!

v. 5 – *"And thou shalt love the LORD thy God with all thine heart, and with all thy soul, and with all thy might."*

    (1) INTIMATE – *"with all thine heart"*

>> **(2) INTENSE** – *"with all thy might"*

5. BELIEVE GOD! We need a personal RESPONSE to God's word – *"these words, which I command thee this day, shall be in thine heart"*

>> **(1) It gives STABILITY in your life!**

Psalm 37:23-24 – *"The steps of a good man are ordered by the LORD, and he delighteth in His way. Though he fall, he shall not be utterly cast down; for the LORD upholdeth him with His hand."*

Psalm 37:31 – *"The law of his God is in his heart: none of his steps shall slide."*

(2) It causes <u>SUCCESS</u> in your walk with the LORD!

Joshua 1:8-9 – *"This book of the law shall not depart out of thy mouth, but thou shalt meditate therein day and night, that thou mayest observe to do according to all that is written therein; for then thou shalt make thy way prosperous, and then thou shalt have good success."*

Psalm 1:1-3 – *"Blessed is the man who walketh not in the counsel of the ungodly, nor standeth in the way of sinners, nor sitteth in the seat of the scornful. But his delight is in the law of the LORD; and in His law doth he meditate day and night. And he shall be like a tree planted by the rivers of water, that bringeth forth its fruit in its season; its leaf also shall not* *wither; and whatsoever he doeth shall prosper."*

   (3) It brings **STRENGTH** in your struggled with sin!

Psalm 119:9-11 – *"Wherewithal shall a young men cleanse his way? By taking heed thereto according to Thy word. With my whole heart have I sought Thee; Oh, let me not wander from Thy commandments. Thy word have I hidden in mine heart, that I might not sin against Thee."*

6. SERVE GOD! **We need a definite responsibility toward our family!**

Zechariah 6:7-9 – *"And thou shalt teach them diligently unto thy children, and shalt talk of them when thou sittest in thine house, and when thou walkest by the* *way, and when thou liest down, and when thou risest up. And thou shalt bind them for a sign upon thine hand, and they shall be as frontlets between thine eyes. And thou shalt write them upon the posts of thy house, and on thy gates."*

(1) <u>TEACH</u> your children diligently!

(2) <u>TALK</u> to your children continually!

(3) <u>TELL</u> your children what God has done for you!

(4) <u>TRAIN</u> your children in the way of the LORD!

Proverbs 22:6 – *"Train up a child in the way he should go and, when* *he is old, he will not depart from it."*

7. <u>REMEMBER GOD!</u> We need a continual REMINDER of what God has done and will do!

Deuteronomy 6:10-12 – *"And it shall be, when the LORD thy God shall have brought thee into the land which He swore unto thy fathers, to Abraham, to Isaac, and to Jacob, to give thee great and goodly cities, which thou buildedst not, and houses full of all good things, which thou filledst not, and wells digged, which thou diggedst not, vineyards and olive trees, which thou plantedst not, when thou shalt have eaten and be full; Then beware lest thou forget the LORD, Who brought thee forth out of the land of Egypt, from the house of bondage."*

Deuteronomy 8:2 – *"And thou shalt remember all the way which the LORD thy God led thee these forty years in the wilderness, to humble thee, and to prove thee, to know what was in thine heart, whether thou wouldest keep His commandments, or not."*

Deuteronomy 8:11 – *"Beware that thou forget not the LORD thy God, in not keeping His commandments, and His judgments, and His statutes, which I command thee this day."*

The <u>CHOOSING</u> of Israel as the people of God!
Deuteronomy 7:1-26

The <u>COMMAND</u> of the LORD to Israel regarding the seven nations — Deuteronomy 7:1-5

"When the LORD thy God shall bring thee into the land where thou goest to possess it, and hath cast out many nations before thee, the Hittites, and the Girgashites, and the Amorites, and the Canaanites, and the Perizzites, and the Hivites, and the Jebusites, seven nations greater and mightier than thou, and when the LORD thy God shall deliver them before thee, thou shalt smite them, and utterly destroy them; thou shalt make no covenant with them, nor show mercy unto them. Neither shalt thou make

marriages with them; thy daughter thou shalt not give unto his son, nor his daughter shalt thou take unto thy son. For they will turn away thy son from following Me, that they may serve other gods; so will the anger of the LORD be kindled against you, and destroy thee suddenly. But thus shall ye deal with them: ye shall destroy their altars, and break down their images, and cut down their groves, and burn their graven images with fire."

1. The **PROMISE** of God to cast out these nations – *"seven nations greater and mightier than thou"*

2. The **PUNISHMENT** that Israel must bring upon these nations – *"thou shalt smite them, and utterly destroy them"*

3. The **PROHIBITIONS** they must honor – vv. 2b-4

    (1) No **COVENANT** with them!

    (2) No **COMPASSION** for them!

    (3) No **COMPANIONSHIP** with them!

    (4) No **COMPROMISE** with them!

4. The **POLLUTIONS** they must destroy! v. 5

The **CHOICE** of Israel as the people of God –
Deuteronomy 7:6-11

"But thou art an holy people unto the LORD thy God; the LORD thy God hath chosen thee to be a special people unto Himself,

above all people who are upon the face of the earth. The LORD did not set His love upon you, nor choose you, because ye were more in number than any people; for ye were the fewest of all people. But because the LORD loved you, and because He would keep the oath which He had sworn unto your fathers, hath the LORD brought you out with mighty hand, and redeemed you out of the house of bondmen, from the hand of Pharoah, king of Egypt. Know, therefore, that the LORD thy God, He is God, the faithful God, Who keepeth covenant and mercy with them who love Him and keep His commandments to a thousand generations, and repayeth them who hate Him to their face, to destroy them; He will not be slack to him who hateth Him; He will repay him to his face. Thou shalt, therefore, keep the commandments, and the statutes, and the judgments, which I command thee this day, to do them."

1. A <u>SEPARATED</u> people – *"holy people unto the LORD thy God"*

2. A <u>SPECIAL</u> people – *"the LORD thy God hath chosen thee to be a special people unto Himself, above all people that are ;upon the face of the earth"*

3. A <u>SELECTED</u> people – *"Because the LORD love you, and because He would keep the oath which He had sworn unto your fathers"*

    (1) Based on His <u>LOVE</u>!

(2) Based on His **FAITHFULNESS!**

4. A **SAVED** people – *"redeemed you out of the house of bondmen"*

    (1) Based on the **CHARACTER** of God Himself! *"the faithful God"*

    (2) Based on the **COMMANDMENTS** they will keep!

The **CONSEQUENCES** they will experience as the people of God!
Deuteronomy 7:12-26

1. The **PROMISE** of the covenant will be fulfilled!

v. 12 – *"Wherefore it shall come to pass, if ye hearken to these judgments, and keep, and do them, that the LORD thy God shall keep unto thee the covenant and the mercy which He swore unto thy fathers."*

2. Their <u>PRODUCTIVITY</u> will increase! vv. 13-14

"And He will love thee, and bless thee, and multiply thee; He will also bless the fruit of thy womb, and the fruit of thy land, thy corn, and thy wine, and thine oil, the increase of thy kine, and the flocks of thy sheep, in the land which He swore unto thy fathers to give thee. Thou shalt be blessed above all people; there shall not be male or female barren among you, or among your cattle."

3. Their <u>PROSPERITY</u> will be seen in their good health – v. 15

"And the LORD will take away from thee all sickness, and will put none of the evil diseases of Egypt, which thou knowest, upon thee, but will lay them upon all those who hate thee."

    4. The **PUNISHMENT** of foreign nations is guaranteed! vv. 16-26

        (1)   The **DELIVERANCE** of the LORD is promised! vv. 16, 23-24

"the LORD thy God shall deliver thee"

        (2)   Their total **DESTRUCTION** is predicted! vv. 16, 20, 22-24

        (3)   The **DEFILEMENT** of false religion and

idolatry shall not be tolerated! vv. 16, 25-26

"neither shall thou serve their gods; for that will be a snare unto thee"

    (4)   Their <u>DEFENSE</u> is based on the mighty power of God! vv. 17-19, 21

"Thou shalt not be affrighted at them; for the LORD thy God is among you, a mighty God and terrible."

The <u>CAUTION</u> of the Lord –

Deuteronomy 8:1-20

The <u>REASON</u> behind the LORD's caution – v. 1

"All the commandments which I command thee this day shall ye observe to do, that ye may live, and multiply, and go in and possess the land which the LORD swore to give unto your fathers."

The <u>REMEMBRANCE</u> of how the LORD guided them through the wilderness – vv. 2-5

"And thou shalt remember all the way which the LORD thy God led thee these forty years in the wilderness, to humble thee, and to prove thee, to know what was in

thine heart, whether thou wouldest keep His commandments or not. And He humbled thee, and suffered thee to hunger, and fed thee with manna, which thou knewest not, neither did thy fathers know; that He might make thee know that man doth not live by bread only, but by every word that proceedeth out of the mouth of the LORD doth man live. The raiment waxed not old upon thee, neither did thy foot swell, these forty years. Thou shalt also consider in thine heart, that, as a man chasteneth his son, so the LORD thy God chasteneth thee."

1. The **PERIOD** of time involved – *"these 40 years in the wilderness"*

2. The **PURPOSE** which the LORD had – *"to humble thee,*

and to prove thee, to know what was in thine heart."

3. The <u>PROVISION</u> for their every need – *"fed thee with manna"* – *"The raiment waxed not old upon thee, neither did thy foot swell, these 40 years"*

It was this passage that Yeshua referred to in the temptation attempts of Satan.

Matthew 4:1-4 – *"Then was Yeshua (Jesus) led up by the Spirit into the wilderness to be tempted by the devil. And when He had fasted forty days and forty nights, He was afterward an hungred. And when the tempter came to Him, he said, If Thou be the Son of God, command that these stones be made bread. But He answered and said, It is written, Man shall not live by bread alone, but by every word that proceedeth out of the mouth of God."*

4. The <u>PURIFYING</u> of His people – v. 5 – *"so the LORD thy God chasteneth thee"*

Hebrews 12:5-7 – *"And ye have forgotten the exhortation which speaketh unto you as unto children, My son, despise not thou the chastening of the LORD, nor faint when thou art rebuked of Him; For whom the LORD loveth He chasteneth, and scourgeth every son whom He receiveth. If ye endure chastening, God dealeth with you as with sons; for what son is he whom the father chasteneth not?*

Hebrews 12:11 – *"Now no chastening for the present seemeth to be joyous, but grievous; nevertheless, afterward it yieldeth the peaceable fruit of*

righteousness unto them who are exercise by it."

The <u>RESPONSE</u> of blessing which the LORD will bring when we are obedient to Him!

vv. 6-10 – *"Therefore thou shalt keep the commandments of the LORD thy God, to walk in His ways, and to fear Him. For the LORD thy God bringeth thee into a good land, a land of brooks of water, of fountains and depths that spring out of valleys and hills; A land of wheat, and barely, and vines, and fig trees, and pomegranates; a land of olive oil, and honey; A land wherein thou shalt eat bread without scarceness; thou shalt not lack anything in it; a land whose stones are iron, and out of whose hills thou mayest dig brass. When thou hast eaten and art full, then* *thou shalt bless the LORD thy God for the good land which He hath given thee."*

1. The **PRACTICE** of obedience involves two issues – v. 6

    (1) Our **APPLICATION** of His ways – *"to walk in His ways"*

    (2) Our **ACCOUNTABILITY** to Him – *"to fear Him"*

2. The **PROSPERITY** which God will bring – vv. 7-9

    (1) Available supply of water

    (2) Agricultural diversity

    (3) Abundant provision – *"thou*

shalt not lack any thing in it"

3. The <u>PRAISE</u> we should give to God – v. 10 – *"thou shalt bless the LORD thy God for the good land which He hath given thee."*

The <u>RECOGNITION</u> of the LORD's supply can be easily forgotten – vv. 11-18

1. The <u>PROBLEM</u> arises when we are being materially blessed! vv. 11-13

"Beware that thou forget not the LORD thy God, in not keeping His commandments, and His judgments, and His statutes, which I command thee this day, Lest, when thou hast eaten and art full and hast built goodly houses, and dwelt therein; And

when thy herds and thy flocks multiply, and thy silver and thy gold are multiplied, and all that thou hast is multiplied."

2. The <u>**PRIDE**</u> that forgets how the LORD has taken care of us – vv. 14-16

"Then thine heart be lifted up, and thou forget the LORD thy God, Who brought thee forth out of the land of Egypt, from the house of bondage; Who led thee through that great and terrible wilderness, wherein were fiery serpents, and scorpions, and drought, where there was no water; Who brought thee forth water out of the rock of flint: Who fed thee in the wilderness with manna, which thy fathers knew not, that He might humble thee, and that He might prove thee, to do thee good at thy latter end."

- (1) He **DELIVERED** from bondage – v. 14

- (2) He **DIRECTED** their paths in the wilderness – v. 15

- (3) He **DEVELOPED** their trust in Him – v. 16

3. The **PERSPECTIVE** that we lose when we forget what the LORD has done – vv. 17-18

- (1) We begin to take **CREDIT** for what the LORD has done!

- (2) We forget that it is His **COVENANT** behind it all!

The **RESULT** which God will cause if we are disobedient! vv. 19-20

"And it shall be, if thou do at all forget the LORD thy God, and walk after other gods, and serve them, and worship them, I testify against you this day that ye shall utterly perish. As the nations which the LORD destroyeth before your face, so shall ye perish, because ye would not be obedient unto the voice of the LORD your God."

   1. Our **DESTRUCTION** – v. 19
      "ye shall surely perish"

   2. Our **DISOBEDIENCE** – v. 20
      "because ye would not be obedient unto the voice of the LORD your God"

The **CLEANSING** of His people – Deuteronomy 9:1-29

The **REASON** why the LORD God gave the Land to Israel – vv. 1-6

"Hear, O Israel: Thou art to pass over the Jordan this day, to go in to possess nations greater and mightier than thyself, cities great and fenced up to heaven, A people great and tall, the children of the Anakim, whom thou knowest, and of whom thou hast heard say, who can stand before the children of Anak! Understand, therefore, this day, that the LORD thy God is He Who goeth over before thee; as a consuming fire He shall destroy them, and He shall bring them down before thy face. So shalt

thou drive them out, and destroy them quickly, as the LORD hath said unto thee. Speak not thou in thine heart, after the LORD thy God hath cast them out from before thee, saying, For my righteousness the LORD hath brought me in to possess this land; but for the wickedness of these nations the LORD doth drive them out from before thee. Not for thy righteousness, nor for the uprightness of thine heart, dost thou go to possess their land, but for the wickedness of these nations the LORD thy God doth drive them out from before thee, and that He may perform the word which the LORD swore unto thy fathers, Abraham, Isaac, and Jacob. Understand, therefore, that the LORD thy God giveth thee not this good land to possess for thy righteousness; for thou art a stiff-necked people."

1. The **OBSTACLES** would be great!

    (1) As to **NATIONS** – *"greater and mightier than thyself"*

    (2) As to **CITIES** – *"great and fenced up to heaven"*

    (3) As to **PEOPLE** – *"a people great and tall, the children of the Anakims"*

2. The **OUTCOME** would be determined by the LORD – v. 3 – *"a consuming fire He shall destroy them"*

3. The **OBJECTIVE** would be made clear – vv. 4-6a – *"not*

for thy righteousness...but for the wickedness of these nations"

4. The <u>ORIGIN</u> of their problem – v. 6b – *"a stiff-necked people"*

The <u>REBELLION</u> which they manifested in the wilderness – vv. 7-24

1. They <u>PROVOKED</u> the LORD to wrath continually – v. 7

"Remember, and forget not, how thou provokedst the LORD thy God to wrath in the wilderness; from the day that thou didst depart out of the land of Egypt, until ye came unto this place, ye have been rebellious against the LORD."

2. They <u>POLLUTED</u> themselves at Mount Horeb – vv. 8-12

"Also in Horeb ye provoked the LORD to wrath, so that the LORD was angry with you to have destroyed you. When I was gone up into the mount to receive the tables of stone, even the tables of the covenant which the LORD made with you, then I abode in the mount forty days and forty nights; I neither did eat bread not drink water. And the LORD delivered unto me two tables of stone written with the finger of God; and on them was written according to all the words which the LORD spoke with you in the mount out of the midst of the fire in the day of the assembly. And it came to pass at the end of forty days and forty nights, that the LORD gave me the two tables of stone, even the tables of the covenant. And the LORD said unto me, Arise, get thee down

quickly from here; for thy people whom thou hast brought out of Egypt have corrupted themselves. They are quickly turned aside out of the way which I commanded them; they have made them a molten image."

    3. They <u>PROVED</u> they deserved the judgment of the LORD God – vv. 13-17 – *"I have seen this people"*

        (1) Their <u>ATTITUDES</u> were clear – v. 13 – *"it is a stiff-necked people"*

        (2) The <u>ANGER</u> of the LORD was fully justified – vv. 24-26

"Ye have been rebellious against the LORD from the day that I knew you. Thus I fell down before the LORD forty days and forty

nights, as I fell down at the first, because the LORD had said He would destroy you. I prayed, therefore, unto the LORD, and said, O Lord GOD, destroy not Thy people and Thine inheritance, whom Thou hast redeemed through Thy greatness, whom Thou hast brought forth out of Egypt with a mighty hand."

    (3)   The <u>ACTION</u> of Moses was amazing! v. 17

"And I took the two tables, and cast them out of my two hands, and broke them before your eyes."

  4. Moses <u>PLEADED</u> with God for His mercy – vv. 18-21

    (1)   He <u>HUMBLED</u> himself – v. 18

"because of all your sins"

(2) The LORD HEARKENED unto him – vv. 19-21

"I was afraid of the anger and hot displeasure, wherewith the LORD was wroth against you to destroy you"

v. 20 – "And I prayed for Aaron also the same time"

5. The PLACES where their rebellion was manifested – vv. 22-24

"And at Taberah, and at Massah, and at Kibroth-hatta, ye provoked the LORD to wrath. Likewise, when the LORD sent you from Kadesh-barnea, saying, Go up and possess the land which I have given you; then ye rebelled against the commandment of the LORD your God, and ye believed Him not, nor hearkened to His

voice." Ye have been rebellious against the LORD from the day that I knew you."

    (1)   TABERAH – lack of **COMMITMENT** to the plan of God!

    (2)   MASSAH – lack of **CONFIDENCE** in the presence of the LORD!

    (3)   KIBROTH-HATTAAVAH – lack of **CONTENTMENT** in the provision of the LORD!

    (4)   KADESH-BARNEA – lack of **COURAGE** in the power of the LORD!

The RESPONSE of Moses – vv. 25-29

"Thus I fell down before the LORD forty days and forty nights, as I fell down at the first, because the LORD had said He would destroy you. I prayed, therefore, unto the LORD, and said, O Lord GOD, destroy not Thy people and Thine inheritance, whom Thou hast redeemed through Thy greatness, whom Thou hast brought forth out of Egypt with a mighty hand. Remember Thy servants, Abraham, Isaac, and Jacob; look not unto the stubbornness of this people, nor to their wickedness, nor to their sin, Lest the land from which Thou broughtest us out say, Because the LORD was not able to bring them into the land which He promised them, and because He hated them, He hath brought them out to slay them in the wilderness. Yet they are Thy people and Thine inheritance,

whom Thou broughtest out by Thy mighty power and by Thine stretched out arm."

1. Based on His <u>REDEMPTION</u> of His people – v. 26

2. Based on His <u>REMEMBRANCE</u> of His servants – v. 27

3. Based on the <u>REACTION</u> of others – v. 28

4. Based on the <u>RELATIONSHIP</u> which He had with them – v. 29 – *"they are Thy people and Thine inheritance"*

The second set of COMMANDMENTS

Deuteronomy 10:1-22

The <u>DELIVERY</u> of the second set of commandments – vv. 1-5

"At that time the LORD said unto me, Hew thee two tables of stone like unto the first, and come up unto me into the mount, and make thee an ark of wood. And I will write on the tables the words that were in the first tables which thou didst break, and thou shalt put them in the ark. And I made an ark of Shittim wood, and hewed two tables of stone like unto the first, and went up into the mount, having the two tables in mine hand. And He wrote on the tables, according to the first writing, the

ten commandments, which the LORD spoke unto you in the mount out of the midst of the fire in the day of the assembly; and the LORD gave them unto me. And I turned myself and came down from the mount, and put the tables in the ark which I had made; and there they are, as the LORD commanded me."

1. A <u>REMINDER</u> of what the LORD said to Moses – vv. 1-3

2. A <u>RESPONSE</u> from Moses was based on the LORD's command to him – vv. 4-5

The <u>DIRECTION</u> in which Israel took their journey from Mt. Horeb –
vv. 6-11

1. The <u>PLACE</u> where Aaron died and was buried – v. 6

"And the children of Israel took their journey from Beeroth Benejaakan to Moserah; there Aaron died, and there he was buried, and Eleazar, his son, ministered in the priest's office in his stead."

> 2. The **PROVISION** of water – v. 7 – *"from there they journeyed unto Gudgodah; and from Gudgodah to Jotbathah, a land of rivers of water"*
>
> 3. The **POSITION** of the tribe of Levi – vv. 8-9

"At that time the LORD separated the tribe of Levi, to bear the ark of the covenant of the LORD, to stand before the LORD to minister unto Him, and to bless in His NAME, unto this day. Wherefore Levi hath no part nor inheritance with his brethren; the LORD is his

inheritance, according as the LORD thy God promised him.

> (1) To **BEAR** the ark!
>
> (2) To **BLESS** in His NAME!

4. The **PRAYER** of Moses for the people – v. 10 – *"And I stayed in the mount, according to the first time, forty days and forty nights; and the LORD hearkened unto me at that time also, and the LORD would not destroy thee."*

5. The **PLAN** of God for the people – v. 11 – *"And the LORD said unto me, Arise, take thy journey before the people that they may go in and possess the land which I swore unto their fathers to give unto them."*

The <u>DEMAND</u> to be circumcised in heart!
vv. 12-22

1. The <u>REQUIREMENTS</u> of the LORD for His people – vv. 12-13

"And now, Israel, what doth the LORD thy God require of thee, but to fear the LORD thy God, to walk in all His ways, and to love Him, and to serve the LORD thy God with all thy heart and with all thy soul."

    (1) <u>ACCOUNTABILITY</u> to God – *"fear the LORD thy God"*

    (2) <u>ACCEPTANCE</u> of His ways – *"walk in all His ways"*

(3) **AFFECTION** for Him – *"and to love Him"*

(4) **AVAILABILITY** to Him – *"serve the LORD thy God"*

(5) **APPLICATION** of His commands – *"keep the commandments of the LORD, and His statutes which I command thee this day for thy good"*

2. The **RECOGNITION** of the LORD's greatness – v. 14

"Behold, the heaven and the heaven of heavens belong to the LORD thy God, the earth also, with all that therein is."

3. The <u>RELATIONSHIP</u> the LORD has with His people – v. 15

"Only the LORD had a delight in thy fathers to love them, and He chose their seed after them, even you above all people, as it is this day."

4. The <u>RESPONSE</u> that the LORD wants from His people – vv. 16-21

   (1) CIRCUMCISION OF THE HEART!

v. 16 - *"Circumcise, therefore, the foreskin of your heart, and be no more stiff-necked"*

<u>NOTE:</u> Circumcision physically refers to the cutting off of the foreskin of the male organ. Figuratively it refers to those who are Jews in contrast to Gentiles.

Spiritually, it refers to repentance and faith in the LORD Himself!

> **(2) COMPASSION for the stranger – vv. 18-19**

"He doth execute the judgment of the fatherless and widow, and loveth the stranger, in giving him food and raiment. Love ye, therefore, the stranger; for ye were strangers in the land of Egypt."

> **(3) COMMITMENT to the LORD Himself – v. 20**

"Thou shalt fear the LORD thy God; Him shalt thou serve, and to Him shalt thou cleave, and swear by His NAME.'

> **(4) CONSIDERATION of all He has done for us – v. 21**

"He is thy praise, and He is thy God, Who hath done for thee these great and terrible things which thine eyes have seen."

The <u>REMEMBRANCE</u> of how He has blessed them!
v. 22

"Thy fathers went down into Egypt with threescore and ten persons, and now the LORD thy God hath made thee as the stars of heaven for multitude."

The <u>CARE</u> of the Land
(Deuteronomy 11:1-32)

The <u>REQUIREMENTS</u> for taking possession of the Land – vv. 1-9

1. <u>LOVE</u> the LORD thy God – v. 1a – *"Therefore, thou shalt love the LORD thy God"*

2. <u>LISTEN</u> always to what He commands – vv. 1b, 8

"and keep His charge, and His statutes, and His judgments, and His commandments always"

3. <u>LEARN</u> from all that your eyes have seen – vv. 2-7 – *"know ye this day"*

    (1) His <u>CHASTISEMENT</u> v. 2

"And know ye this day (for I speak not with your children who have not known, and who have not seen the chastisement of the LORD your God) His greatness, His mighty hand, and His stretched out arm"

> (2) His <u>CONQUEST</u> of Pharaoh and Egypt – vv. 3-4

"And His miracles, and His acts, which He did in the midst of Egypt unto Pharaoh, the kind of Egypt, and unto his land; And what He did unto the army of Egypt, unto their horses, and to their chariots; how He made the water of the Red Sea to overflow them as they pursued after you, and how the LORD hath destroyed them unto this day."

(3) His <u>CARE</u> during their wilderness wanderings – v. 5

"And what He did unto you in the wilderness, until ye came into this place"

(4) His <u>CONSEQUENCE</u> upon those who rebelled – v. 6

"And what He did unto Dathan and Abiram, the sons of Eliab, the son of Reuben – how the earth opened its mouth and swallowed them up, and their households, and their tents, and all the substance that was in their possession, in the midst of all Israel."

The **RECOGNITION** of how different the promised Land would be – vv. 10-12

"But the Land, to which ye go to possess it, is not as the land of Egypt, from where ye came out, where thou sowedst thy seed, and wateredst it with thy foot, as a garden of herbs. But the Land, to which ye go to possess it, is a Land of hills and valleys, and drinketh water of the rain of heaven, a Land which the LORD thy God careth for. The eyes of the LORD thy God are always upon it, from the beginning of the year even unto the end of the year."

1. A **CONTRAST** to the land of Egypt – *"not as the land of Egypt"*

2. A <u>CONTAINER</u> of the water of heaven – *"drinketh water of the rain of heaven"*

3. A <u>CARING</u> from the LORD God Himself – *"A Land which the LORD thy God careth for; the eyes of the LORD thy God are always upon it."*

The <u>REALIZATION</u> of what could easily happen to them – vv. 13-17

1. When you are <u>DILIGENT</u> with His commandments – vv. 13-15

"And it shall come to pass, if ye shall hearken diligently unto My commandments which I command you this day, to love the LORD your God, and to serve Him with all your heart and with all your soul. That I will give you the rain

of your Land in its due season, the first rain and the latter rain, that thou mayest gather in thy corn, and thy wine, and thine oil. And I will send grass in thy fields for thy cattle, that thou mayest eat and be full."

    2. When you are <u>DECEIVED</u> – vv. 16-17

"Take heed to yourselves, that your heart be not deceived, and ye turn aside, and serve other gods, and worship them; And then the LORD's wrath be kindled against you, and He shut up the heaven, that there be no rain, and that the Land yield not her fruit; and lest ye perish quickly from off the good Land which the LORD giveth you."

        (1)   Your <u>WORSHIP</u> has changed – *"ye turn aside, and*

serve other gods, and worship them."

(2) His <u>WRATH</u> will come – *"ye perish quickly from off the good Land which the LORD giveth you"*

The <u>RESPONSIBILITY</u> they must have for their family – vv. 18-21

"Therefore shall ye lay up these My words in your heart and in your soul, and bind them for a sign upon your hand, that they may be as frontlets between your eyes. And ye shall teach them to your children, speaking of them when thou sittest in thine house, and when thou walkest by the way, when thou liest down, and

when thou risest up. And thou shalt write them upon the doorposts of thine house, and upon thy gates. That your days may be multiplied, and the days of your children, in the Land which the LORD swore unto your fathers to give them, as the days of heaven upon the earth."

1. <u>TREASURE</u> them in your heart and soul – v. 18a

2. <u>TIE</u> them on your hand and between your eyes – v. 18b

3. <u>TEACH</u> them to your children – v. 19a

4. <u>TALK</u> about them in your house – v. 19b

5. <u>TAKE</u> them in writing to your door and your gates – v. 20

6. <u>TRUST</u> the promises of the LORD for your family – v. 21

The **REACTION** of the LORD toward all the nations that will face in the future – vv. 22-25

1. Your **DILIGENCE** will give you victory – v. 22

"For if ye shall diligently keep all these commandments which I command you, to do them, to love the LORD your God, to walk in all His ways, and to cleave unto Him"

2. The **DRIVING OUT** of nations greater and mightier than yourselves – v. 23

"Then will the LORD drive out all these nations from before you, and ye shall possess greater nations and mightier than yourselves."

3. The **DIMENSIONS** of what you will conquer – v. 24

"Every place whereon the soles of your feet shall tread shall be yours: from the wilderness and Lebanon, from the river, the river Euphrates, even unto the uttermost sea shall your coast be."

    4. The <u>DREAD</u> of you will come to all the Land – v. 25

"There shall no man be able to stand before you; for the LORD your God shall lay the fear of you and the dread of you upon all the land that ye shall tread upon, as He hath said unto you."

The <u>RESULTS</u> they will face in terms of blessings and curses – vv. 26-32

"Behold, I set before you this day a blessing and a curse"

1. A <u>BLESSING</u> if they obey – v. 27

"A blessing, if ye obey the commandments of the LORD your God, which I command you this day"

2. A <u>CURSE</u> if they disobey – vv. 28-29

"And a curse, if ye will not obey the commandments of the LORD your God, but turn aside out of the way which I command you this day, to go after other gods, which ye have not known. And it shall come to pass, when the LORD thy God hath brought thee in unto the Land to which thou goest to possess it, that thou shalt put the blessing upon Mount Gerizim, and the curse upon Mount Ebal."

POSSESSION OF THE LAND OF THE CANAANITES – vv. 30-32

"Are they not on the other side of the Jordan, by the way where the sun goeth down, in the land of the Canaanites, who dwell in the Arabah over against Gilgal, beside the plains of Moreh? For ye shall pass over the Jordan to go in to possess it, and dwell therein. And ye shall observe to do all the statutes and judgments which I set before you this day."

The <u>CHOICE</u> of the places God has chosen – Deuteronomy 12:1-32

II Chronicles 6:6 – *"But I have chosen Jerusalem, that My NAME might be there; and have chosen David to be over My people Israel."*

Psalm 76:2 – *"In Salem also is His tabernacle, and His dwelling place in Zion."*

Psalm 132:13-14 – *"For the LORD hath chosen Zion; He hath desired it for habitation. This is My rest forever; here will I dwell, for I have desired it."*

Psalm 135:21 – *"Blessed be the LORD out of Zion, which dwelleth* at Jerusalem. Praise ye the LORD."

Their **RESPONSIBILITIES** in the place God has chosen — Deuteronomy 12:1-16

   1. The **COMMANDMENTS** are to be observed — v. 1

"These are the statutes and judgments which ye shall observe to do in the Land, which the LORD God of thy fathers giveth thee to possess, all the days that ye live upon the earth."

   2. The **CORRUPTION** of idolatry must be destroyed — vv. 2-4

"Ye shall utterly destroy all the places wherein the nations which ye shall possess served their gods, upon the high mountains, and upon the hills, and under every green tree; And ye shall

overthrown their altars, and break their pillars, and burn their groves with fire; and ye shall hew down the graven images of their gods, and destroy the names of them out of that place. Ye shall not do so unto the LORD your God."

   3. The <u>COMMITMENT</u> to worship with your sacrifices and tithes shall be observed – vv. 5-6

"But unto the place which the LORD your God shall choose out of all your tribes to put His NAME there, even unto His habitation shall ye seek, and there thou shalt come; And there ye shall bring your burnt offerings, and your sacrifices, and your tithes, and heave offerings of your hand, and your vows, and your freewill

offerings, and the firstlings of your herds and of your flocks."

    4. The <u>CAUSE</u> for rejoicing – v. 7

"And there ye shall eat before the LORD your God, and ye shall rejoice in all that ye put your hand unto, ye and your households, wherein the LORD thy God hath blessed thee."

    5. The <u>CAUTION</u> to God's people – vv. 8-9

"Ye shall not do after all the things that we do here this day, every man whatsoever is right in his own eyes. For ye are not as yet come to the rest and to the inheritance which the LORD your God giveth you."

    6. The <u>COMING</u> over Jordan – vv. 10-16

"But when ye go over the Jordan, and dwell in the Land which the LORD your God giveth you to inherit, and when He giveth you rest from all your enemies round about, so that ye dwell in safety, Then there shall be a place which the LORD your God shall choose to cause His NAME to dwell there; there shall ye bring all that I command you: your burnt offerings, and your sacrifices, your tithes, and the heave offering of your hand, and all your choice vows which ye vow unto the LORD. And ye shall rejoice before the LORD your God, ye, and your sons, and your daughters, and your menservants, and your maidservants, and the Levite who is within your gates, forasmuch as he hath no part nor inheritance with you. Take heed to thyself that thou offer not thy burnt

offerings in every place that thou seest; But in the place which the LORD shall choose in one of thy tribes, there thou shalt offer thy burnt offerings, and there thou shalt do all that I command thee. Notwithstanding, thou mayest kill and eat flesh in all thy gates. Whatsoever thy soul lusteth after, according to the blessing of the LORD thy God, which He hath given thee: the unclean and the clean may eat thereof, as of the roebuck, and as of the hart. Only ye shall not eat the blood; ye shall pour it upon the earth as water."

7. The <u>CONSUMING</u> of food – vv. 17-19

"Thou mayest not eat within thy gates of thy corn, or of thy wine, or of thy oil, or the firstlings of thy herds or of thy flock, nor any of thy vows which thou vowest,

nor thy freewill offerings, or heave offering of thine hand; But thou must eat them before the LORD thy God in the place which the LORD thy God shall choose, thou, and thy son, and thy daughter, and thy manservant, and thy maidservant, and the Levite who is within thy gates; and thou shalt rejoice before the LORD thy God in all that thou puttest thine hands unto. Take heed to thyself that thou forsake not the Levite as long as thou livest upon the earth."

8. The <u>CHOICES</u> about the food of God's people – vv. 20-28

"When the LORD thy God shall enlarge thy border, as He hath promised thee, and thou shalt say, I will eat flesh, because they soul longeth to eat flesh, thou mayest eat flesh, whatsoever thy soul

lusteth after. If the place which the LORD thy God hath chosen to put His NAME be too far from thee, then thou shalt kill of thy herd and of thy flock, which the LORD hath given thee, as I have commanded thee, and thou shalt eat in thy gates whatsoever thy soul lusteth after. Even as the roebuck and the hart is eaten, so thou shalt eat them: the unclean and the clean shall eat of them alike. Only be sure that thou eat not the blood; for the blood is the life, and thou mayest not eat the life with the flesh. Thou shalt not eat it; thou shalt pour it upon the earth as water. Thou shalt not eat it, that it may go well with thee, and with thy children after thee, when thou shalt do that which is right in the sight of the LORD. Only the holy things which thou hast, and thy vows, thou shalt take, and go unto the place which the LORD shall choose. And thou shalt offer thy burnt offerings, the flesh and the blood, upon the altar of the LORD thy God; and the blood of thy sacrifices shall be poured out upon the altar of the LORD thy God, and thou shalt eat the flesh. Observe and hear all these words which I command thee, that it may go well with thee, and thy children after thee forever, when thou doest that which is good and right in the sight of the LORD thy God."

9. The <u>CONDEMNATION</u> of following false gods – vv. 29-32

"When the LORD thy God shall cut off the nations from before thee, where thou goest to possess them, and thou succeedest them, and dwellest in their land, Take heed

to thyself that thou be not snared by following them, after they are destroyed from before thee, and that thou inquire not after their gods, saying, How did these nations serve their gods? Even so will I do likewise. Thou shalt not do so unto the LORD thy God; for every abomination to the LORD, which He hateth, have thy done unto their gods. For even their sons and their daughters they have burned in the fire to their gods. Whatsoever thing I command you, observe to do it; thou shalt not add thereto, nor diminish from it."

The <u>CONFUSION</u> about false prophets
Deuteronomy 13:1-18

The <u>DECEPTION</u> that God's people might face – vv. 1-5

"If there arise among you a prophet, or a dreamer of dreams, and giveth thee a sign or a wonder, and the sign of the wonder come to pass, whereof he spoke unto thee, saying, Let us go after other gods, which thou hast not known, and let us serve them, Thou shalt not hearken unto the words of that prophet, or that dreamer of dreams; for the LORD your God proveth you, to know whether ye love the LORD your God with all your heart and with all your soul. Ye shall walk after the LORD your God, and fear Him, and keep His

commandments, and obey His voice, and ye shall serve Him, and cleave unto Him. And that prophet, or that dreamer of dreams, shall be put to death, because he hath spoken to turn you away from the LORD your God, Who brought you out of the land of Egypt, and redeemed you out of the house of bondage, to thrust thee out of way which the LORD thy God commanded thee to walk in. So shalt thou put the evil away from the midst of thee."

1. The <u>MEANS</u> used to deceive God's people – vv. 1-2 – *"and the sign or the wonder come to pass"*

2. The <u>MOTIVE</u> which the LORD has in allowing these false prophets to influence God's people – v. 3 – *"for the LORD your God proveth you, to*

know whether ye love the LORD your God with all your heart and with all your soul."

3. The <u>MESSAGE</u> we should hear from this situation – v. 4

    (1) We should <u>LIVE</u> the way the LORD wants us to live – *"walk after the LORD your God"*

    (2) We should <u>LOOK</u> to the LORD for accountability – *"fear Him"*

    (3) We should <u>LISTEN</u> to what He commands – *"obey His voice"*

    (4) We should <u>LEARN</u> how we may serve

> Him – *"ye shall serve Him"*
>
> (5) We should **LOVE** Him without any hesitation – *"and cleave unto Him"*
>
> 4. The **MANNER** in which we should deal with the false prophet – v. 5 – *"shall be put to death"*

The **DANGER** which family and friends can cause – vv. 6-11

"If thy brother, the son of thy mother, or thy son, or thy daughter, or the wife of thy bosom, or thy friend who is as thine own soul, entice thee secretly, saying, Let us go and serve other gods, which thou hast not known, thou, nor thy father, Namely, of the gods of the people who are round about you, nigh

unto thee, or far off from thee, from the one end of the earth even unto the other end of the earth, Thou shalt not consent unto him, nor hearken unto him; neither shall thine eye pity him, neither shalt thou spare, neither shalt thou conceal him. But thou shalt surely kill him; thine hand shall be first upon him to put him to death, and afterward the hand of all the people. And thou shalt stone him with stones, that he die, because he hath sought to thrust thee away from the LORD thy God, Who brought thee out of the land of Egypt, from the house of bondage. And all Israel shall hear, and fear, and shall do no more any such wickedness as this is among you."

1. They can <u>ENTICE</u> you secretly – v. 6 – *"Let us go and serve other gods"*

2. You must <u>END</u> your relationship with them - v. 8 – *"Thou shalt not consent unto him, nor hearken unto him"*

3. You must <u>EXECUTE</u> them because they have tried to turn you away from the LORD your God – vv. 9-10

4. It will <u>ENCOURAGE</u> others to never do such a thing – v. 11 – *"and shall do not more any such wickedness"*

The <u>DESTRUCTION</u> which should be brought upon cities that follow false gods!
vv. 12-18

"If thou shalt hear say in one of thy cities, which the LORD thy God hath given thee to dwell there, saying, Certain men, the children of Belial, are gone out

from among you, and have withdrawn the inhabitants of their city, saying, Let us go and serve other gods, which ye have not known, Then shalt thou inquire, and make search, and ask diligently; and, behold, if it be truth, and the thing certain, that such abomination is wrought among you, Thou shalt surely smite the inhabitants of that city with the edge of the sword, destroying it utterly, and all that is therein, and the cattle thereof, with the edge of the sword. And thou shalt gather all the spoil of it into the midst of the street thereof, and shalt burn with fire the city, and all the spoil thereof every whit, for the LORD thy God, and it shall be an heap forever; it shall not be built again. And there shall cleave nought of the cursed thing to thine hand; that the LORD may turn from the fierceness of His anger, and show thee mercy, and have compassion upon thee, and multiply thee, as He hath sworn unto thy fathers, When thou shalt hearken to the voice of the LORD thy God, to keep all His commandments which I command thee this day, to do that which is right in the eyes of the LORD thy God."

1. The <u>IDENTITY</u> of those who try to persuade you to serve other gods – v. 13 – *"children of Belial"*

2. The <u>INVESTIGATION</u> that must take place – v. 14 – *"inquire, and make search, and ask diligently"*

3. The <u>IMPACT</u> of smiting such a place – vv. 15-16 – *"for the LORD thy God; and it shall*

be a heap forever; it shall not be built again."

4. The <u>INTENT</u> behind such destruction – vv. 17-18

      (1)   To <u>STOP</u> His fierce anger!

      (2)   To <u>SHOW</u> His mercy and compassion!

      (3)   To <u>STIMULATE</u> us to do what is right!

The **CHARACTER** of their holiness –
Deuteronomy 14:1-29

SEPARATE from pagan practices – 14:1-2

"Ye are the children of the LORD your God; ye shall not cut yourselves, nor make any baldness between your eyes for the dead; For thou art an holy people unto the LORD thy God, and the LORD hath chosen thee to be a peculiar people unto Himself, above all the nations that are upon the earth."

1. The **RELATIONSHIP** they had with the LORD should make a difference – v. 1a – *"Ye are the children of the LORD your God"*

2. The **RESPONSE** they should avoid – v. 1b – *"not cut yourselves, nor make any baldness between your eyes for the dead"*

3. The **REASON** behind this – v. 2

    (1) The **UNIQUENESS** of their relationship to the LORD God – v. 2a – *"For thou art an holy people unto the LORD thy God"*

    (2) The **UNDERSTANDING** of what it means to be chosen of God – v. 2b – *"to be a peculiar people unto Himself above all nations that are upon the earth"*

STAY AWAY from eating unclean animals – vv. 3-21

NOTE: Animals that are allowed to eat are called *"kasher"* which refers to what is "fit" or "proper" to eat. Animals that are not "fit" to eat include those that were torn by other beasts instead of being properly slaughtered. These animals are called *"taref"* which comes from the word *"terefah"*

The entire system of dietary laws is called *"kashrut"* which means "fitness." Regarding health issues, that cannot be proved.

14:3 – *"Thou shalt not eat any abominable thing"* – These animals are called *"to'evah"* and connects them with idolatry and immorality issues.

   1. **LAND** animals – vv. 4-8

(1) PERMITTED – vv. 4-6

"These are the beasts which ye shall eat: the ox, the sheep, and the goat. The hart, and the roebuck and fallow deer, and the wile goat, and the pygarg, and the wild ox, and the chamois. And every beast that parteth the hoof, and cleaveth the cleft into two claws, and cheweth the cud among the beasts, that ye shall eat."

(2) PROHIBITED – vv. 7-8

"Nevertheless these ye shall not eat of them that chew the cud, or of them that divide the cloven hoof: the camel, and the hare, and the coney; for they chew the cud, but divide not the hoof; therefore they are unclean unto you. And the swine, because it divideth the

hoof, yet cheweth not the cud, it is unclean unto you; ye shall not eat of their flesh, nor touch their dead carcasses."

2. <u>WATER</u> animals – vv. 9-10

<u>NOTE:</u> One simple rule – only eat that which has "fins and scales."

3. <u>WINGED</u> animals – vv. 11-20

    (1)   **PERMITTED** – *"all clean birds"*

"kasher" laws include chicken, turkey, duck. goose, sparrow, pigeon, dove, partridge, peacock, quail, and pheasant.

    (2)   **PROHIBITED** – birds of prey and scavengers – 21 types, and *"every creeping thing that flieth"*

4. Animals that <u>DIED</u> – v. 21a – *"give it unto the stranger that is in thy gates"*

5. <u>BOILING</u> animals – v. 21b – *"in mother's milk"* – issue is simply sensitivity to animals

<u>SATISFY</u> your hunger and that of others by doing what the LORD commands – vv. 22-29

1. <u>CONSUME</u> your tithes where God said to do it – vv. 22-23

"Thou shalt truly tithe all the increase of thy see, that the field bringeth forth year by year. And thou shalt eat before the LORD thy God, in the place which He shall choose to place His NAME there, the tithe of thy corn, of thy wine, and of thine oil, and the firstlings of thy herds and of thy flocks, that thou mayest learn to fear the LORD thy God always."

(1) The <u>PLACE</u> He chose – v. 23a – *"in the place which He shall choose to place His NAME there"*

(2) The <u>PURPOSE</u> He had – v. 23b – *"that thou mayest learn to fear the LORD thy God always"*

2. <u>CHANGE</u> your tithes into money when you can't bring them – vv. 24-26

"And if the way be too long for thee, so that thou art not able to carry it, or if the place be too far from thee, which the LORD thy God shall choose to set His NAME there, when the LORD thy God hath blessed thee, Then shalt thou turn it into money, and bind up the money in thine hand, and shalt go unto the place which the LORD thy God shall choose. And thou shalt bestow that money for

whatsoever thy soul lusteth after: and thou shalt rejoice, thou, and thine household."

    (1)   The **REASONS** for this exchange – v. 24 – *"thou art not able to carry it; or if the place be too far from thee"*

    (2)   The **REALIZATION** of what you can buy for your tithes – v. 26a – *"whatsoever thy soul lusteth after"*

    (3)   The **REJOICING** that is to take place – v. 26b – *"thou shalt rejoice, thou, and thine household"*

3. **CARE** for the Levites – v. 27 – *"thou shalt not forsake him"*

4. **COMPASSION** for those with special needs – vv. 28-29

"At the end of three years thou shalt bring forth all the tithe of

thine increase the same year, and shalt lay it up within thy gates: And the Levite (because he hath no part nor inheritance with thee), and the stranger, and the fatherless, and the widow, who are within thy gates, shall come, and shall eat and be satisfied; that the LORD thy God may bless thee in all the work of thine hand which thou doest."

(1) **WHEN** you should do it – *"at the end of three years"*

(2) **WHAT** you should bring – *"all the tithe of thine increase the same year"*

(3) **WHO** you should help – *"the Levite, and the stranger, and the fatherless,*

and the widow...within thy gates"

(4) **HOW MUCH should you give –** *"shall eat and be satisfied"*

(5) **WHY should you give it –** *"that the LORD thy God may bless thee in all the work of thine hand which thou doest"*

The <u>CONCERN</u> for the poor –
Deuteronomy 15:1-23

The <u>RELEASE</u> that should happen – vv. 1-6

"At the end of every seven years thou shalt make a release. And this is the manner of the release: every creditor who lendeth ought unto his neighbor shall release it; he shall not exact it of his neighbor, or of his brother, because it is called the LORD's release. Of a foreigner thou mayest exact it again; but that which is thine with thy brother, thine hand shall release, save when there shall be no poor among you; for the LORD shall greatly bless thee in the land which the LORD thy God giveth thee for an inheritance to possess

it, Only if thou carefully hearken unto the voice of the LORD thy God, to observe to do all these commandments which I command thee this day. For the LORD thy God blesseth thee, as He promised thee. And thou shalt lend unto many nations, but thou shalt not borrow; and thou shalt reign over many nations, but they shall not reign over thee."

1. The <u>EVENT</u> that takes place – v. 1 – *"at the end of every seven years thou shalt make a release"*

2. The <u>EXPECTATION</u> of those who received the loan – v. 2 – *"Every creditor that lendeth aught unto his neighbor shall release it; he shall not exact it of his neighbor, or of his brother."*

3. The **EXCEPTIONS** to such an event – vv. 3-4

   (1) The **ACCOUNTABILITY** of the foreigner – v. 3a- *"Of a foreigner thou mayest exact it again"*

   (2) The **ABSENCE** of any poor – v. 4 – *"save when there shall be no poor among you"*

The **RESPONSE** when God blesses you – vv. 5-6

"Only if thou carefully hearken unto the voice of the LORD thy God, to observe to do all these commandments which I command thee this day. For the LORD thy God blesseth thee, as He promised thee. And thou shalt lend unto many nations, but thou shalt not borrow; and thou shalt reign over

many nations, but they shall not reign over thee."

1. <u>LISTEN</u> to God's commands – v. 5

2. <u>LEND</u> but do not borrow – v. 6a

Proverbs 22:7 – *"The rich ruleth over the poor, and the borrower is servant to the lender."*

3. <u>LEAD</u> but do not follow – v. 6b

The <u>REACTION</u> to the poor – vv. 7-11

"If there be among you a poor man of one of thy brethren within any of thy gates in thy Land which the LORD thy God giveth thee, thou shalt not harden thine heart, nor shut thine hand from thy poor brother; But thou shalt open thine hand wide unto him,

and shalt surely lend him sufficient for his need, in that which he wanteth. Beware that there be not a thought in thy wicked heart, saying, The seventh year, the year of release, is at hand; and thine eye be evil against thy poor brother, and thou givest him nought; and he cry unto the LORD against thee, and it be sin unto thee. Thou shalt surely give him, and thine heart shall not be grieved when thou givest unto him, because for this thing the LORD thy God shall bless thee in all thy works, and in all that thou puttest thine hand unto. For the poor shall never cease out of the Land; therefore I command thee, saying, Thou shalt open thine hand wide unto thy brother, to thy poor, and to thy needy, in thy Land."

1. Your <u>HEART</u> should not harden! – v. 7a – *"thou shalt not harden thine heart"*

Proverbs 19:17 – *"He that hath pity upon the poor lendeth unto the LORD; and that which he hath given will he pay him again"*

Proverbs 21:13 – *"Whoso stoppeth his ears at the cry of the poor, he also shall cry himself, but shall not be heard"*

Proverbs 22:22-23 – *"Rob not the poor, because he is poor; neither oppress the afflicted in the gate: For the LORD will plead their cause, and spoil the soul of those that spoiled them"*

2. Your <u>HAND</u> should be opened – vv. 7b-8 – *"thou shalt open thine hand wide upon him, and shalt surely lend him sufficient for his*

need, in that which he wanteth."

Proverbs 28:27 – *"He that giveth unto the poor shall not lack; but he that hideth his eyes shall have many a curse."*

3. Your HELP should not be resisted – vv. 9-11

Proverbs 29:7 – *"The righteous considereth the cause of the poor: but the wicked regardeth not to know it."*

    (1) Don't be UNCONCERNED in your heart and ignore your responsibility – v. 9 *"Beware that there be not a thought in thy wicked heart..."*

    (2) Don't be UPSET about giving –

"thine heart shall be not be grieved"

(3) Don't be **UNAWARE** of how God will bless you – v. 10

Proverbs 22:9 – 'He that hath a bountiful eye shall be blessed; for he giveth of his bread to the poor"

(4) Don't be **UNBELIEVING** about the existence of the poor – v. 11 – "For the poor shall never cease out of the land."

John 12:8 – "For the poor always ye have with you, but Me ye have not always."

The **REDEMPTION** of slaves – vv. 12-18

"And if thy brother, an Hebrew man, or an Hebrew woman, be sold unto thee, and serve thee six years, then in the seventh year thou shalt let him go free from thee. And when thou sendest him out free from thee, thou shalt not let him go away empty. Thou shalt furnish him liberally out of thy flock, and out of thy floor, and out of thy winepress; of that wherewith the LORD thy God hath blessed thee thou shalt give unto him. And thou shalt remember that thou wast a bondman in the land of Egypt, and the LORD thy God redeemed thee; therefore I command thee this thing today. And it shall be, if he say unto thee, I will not go away from thee, because he loveth thee and thine house, because he is well with thee, Then thou shalt take a awl, and thrust it through his ear unto

the door, and he shall be thy servant forever. And also unto thy maidservant thou shalt do likewise. It shall not seem hard unto thee, when thou sendest him away free from thee; for he hath been worth a double hired servant to thee, in serving thee six years; and the LORD thy God shall bless thee in all that thou doest."

1. Don't <u>FORCE</u> a Hebrew slave to work for you longer than six years – v. 12

2. Don't <u>FAIL</u> to give him liberally out of your wealth – vv. 13-14

3. Don't <u>FORGET</u> your slave if he wants to stay with you – vv. 16-18

      (1) The <u>PIERCING</u> of his ear

(2) The **PURPOSE** behind it

(3) The **PROMISE** of the LORD

The **RESPONSIBILITY** of sacrifices – vv. 19-23

"All the firstling males that come of thy herd and of thy flock thou shalt sanctify unto the LORD thy God; thou shalt do no work with the firstling of thy bullock, nor shear the firstling of thy sheep. Thou shalt eat it before the LORD thy God year by year in the place which the LORD shall choose, thou and thy household. And if there be any blemish therein, as if it be lame, or blind, or have any ill blemish, thou shalt not sacrifice it unto the LORD thy God. Thou shalt eat it within thy gates; the unclean and the clean person

shall eat it alike, as the roebuck, and as the hart. Only thou shalt not eat the blood thereof; thou shalt poor it upon the ground as water."

1. The **PROTECTION** of the *"firstling males"* of animals – v. 19

2. The **PLACE** where they are eaten – v. 20

3. The **POLLUTION** that is unacceptable – v. 21

4. The **PRINCIPLES** for eating the sacrifices – v. 22

    ALLOW everyone to participate – *"the unclean and the clean"*

    AVOID eating any blood – v. 23

The **CELEBRATIONS** of Jewish worship
Deuteronomy 16:1-22

The **REASON** for celebrating – v. 1

"Observe the month of Abib and keep the Passover unto the LORD thy God, for in the month of Abib the LORD thy God brought thee forth out of Egypt by night."

The **REQUIREMENTS** for celebrating the Passover – vv. 2-8

1. As to the **PLACE** where it would be celebrated – v. 2b *"in the place which the LORD shall choose to place His NAME there."*

2. As to **PREPARATION** of the bread – vv. 3-4

"Thou shalt eat no leavened bread with it. Seven days shalt thou eat unleavened bread therewith, even the bread of affliction, for thou camest forth out of the land of Egypt in haste, that thou mayest remember the day when thou camest forth out of the land of Egypt all the days of thy life. And there shall be no leavened bread seen with thee in all thy coast seven days; neither shall there anything of the flesh, which thou sacrificedst the first day at evening, remain all night until the morning."

    (1)   **ABSTAIN** from eating any leaven!

    (2)   **APPLY** the words "bread of affliction"

(3) <u>AVOID</u> eating the sacrifice after the Passover night!

4. As to the <u>PRIORITY</u> of the last day – v. 8 – *"on the seventh day shall be a solemn assembly to the LORD thy God: thou shalt do no work therein"*

The <u>REJOICING</u> at the Feast of Weeks (Shavuot or Pentecost) – vv. 9-12

"Seven weeks shalt thou number unto thee: begin to number the seven weeks from such time as thou beginnest to put the sickle to the corn. And thou shalt keep the feast of weeks unto the LORD thy God with a tribute of a freewill offering of thine hand, which thou shalt give unto the LORD thy God, according as the LORD thy God

hath blessed thee. And thou shalt rejoice before the LORD thy God, thou, and thy son, and thy daughter, and thy manservant, and thy maidservant, and the Levite who is within thy gates, and the stranger, and the fatherless, and the widow who are among you in the place which the LORD thy God have chosen to place His NAME there. And thou shalt remember that thou wast a bondman in Egypt. And thou shalt observe and do these statutes."

1. The <u>TIMING</u> – v. 9 – *"Seven weeks shalt thou number unto thee; begin to number the seven weeks from such time as thou beginnest to put the sickle to the corn."*

2. The <u>TRIBUTE</u> involved – v. 10 – "*a tribute* (thank offering)

of a freewill offering of thine hand, which thou shalt give unto the LORD thy God, according as the LORD thy God hath blessed thee."

3. The <u>TEACHING</u> that was done – vv. 11-12

   (1) To <u>REJOICE</u> before the LORD they God! - *"in the place which the LORD thy God hath chosen to place His NAME there"*

   (2) To <u>REMEMBER</u> what it was like in Egypt – *"a bondman in Egypt"*

The <u>REMEMBRANCE</u> of their wilderness wanderings – vv. 13-15

"Thou shalt observe the feast of tabernacles seven days, after thou

hast gathered in thy corn and thy wine. And thou shalt rejoice in thy feast, thou, and thy son, and thy daughter, and thy manservant, and thy maidservant, and the Levite, the stranger, and the fatherless, and the widow who are within thy gates. Seven days shalt thou keep a solemn feast unto the LORD thy God in the place which the LORD shall choose; because the LORD thy God shall bless thee in all thine increase, and in all the works of thine hands; therefore thou shalt surely rejoice."

1. The <u>PLAN</u> for observing it – v. 13 – *"seven days"*

2. The <u>PURPOSE</u> of this celebration – vv. 14-15 – *"thou shalt rejoice"*

A QUICK <u>REVIEW</u> OF THE MAIN TIMES OF CELEBRATION – vv. 16-17

"Three times in a year shall all thy males appear before the LORD thy God in the place which He shall choose: in the feast of unleavened bread, and in the feast of weeks, and in the feast of tabernacles; and they shall not appear before the LORD empty. Every man shall give as he is able, according to the blessing of the LORD thy God which He hath given thee."

1. Their <u>APPEARANCE</u> was required three times a year in Jerusalem – v. 16

2. Their <u>ABILITY</u> was the basis for their gifts – v. 17 – *"according to the blessing of the LORD thy God which He hath given thee."*

The **RESPONSIBILITIES** of leaders – vv. 18-20

"Judges and officers shalt thou make thee in all thy gates, which the LORD thy God giveth thee, throughout thy tribes, and they shall judge the people with just judgment. Thou shalt not wrest judgment. Thou shalt not respect persons, neither take a gift for a gift doth blind the eyes of the wise and pervert the words of the righteous. That which is altogether just shalt thou follow, that thou mayest live and inherit the Land which the LORD thy God giveth thee."

1. The **PRINCIPLES** of justice must be applied – vv. 18-19

     NO **PRACTICES** of twisting judgments!

     NO **PARTIALITY** shown!

NO PERVERTING of judgment by accepting a bribe!

2. The **PURPOSE** of righteous judgments – v. 20 – *"that thou mayest live, and inherit the Land which the LORD thy God giveth thee."*

The **RESISTANCE** to all forms of idolatry – vv. 21-22

1. Don't **CONFUSE** godly worship with pagan practices!

2. Don't **COMPROMISE** godly worship with pagan images!

The **CAREFULNESS** needed in offering sacrifices –

Deuteronomy 17:1-20

BE **CAREFUL** in offering defective sacrifices – v. 1

"Thou shalt not sacrifice unto the LORD thy God any bullock, or sheep, wherein is blemish, or any evil favouredness; for that is an abomination unto the LORD thy God."

Malachi 1:6-8 – *"A son honoreth his father, and a servant his master; If, then, I be a father, where is My honor? And, if I be a master, where is My fear? Saith the LORD of hosts unto you, O priests, that despise My NAME. And ye say, Wherein have we* *despised Thy NAME? Ye offer polluted bread upon Mine altar; and ye say, Wherein have we polluted Thee? In that ye say, The table of the LORD is contemptible. And if ye offer the blind for sacrifice, is it not evil? And if ye offer the lame and sick, is it not evil? Offer it now unto thy governor; will he be pleased with thee, or accept thy person? Saith the LORD of hosts.*

BE <u>CERTAIN</u> ABOUT THE REPORTS OF WICKEDNESS –
vv. 2-7

"If there be found among you, within any of thy gates which the LORD thy God giveth thee, man or woman who hath wrought wickedness in the sight of the LORD thy God, in transgressing

His covenant, And hath gone and served other gods, and worshiped them, either the sun, or moon, or any of the host of heaven, which I have not commanded, And it be told thee, and thou hast heard of it, and inquired diligently, and, behold, it is true, and the thing certain, that such abomination is wrought in Israel; Then shalt thou bring forth that man of that woman, who hath committed that wicked thing, unto thy gates, even that man or that woman, and shalt stone them with stones, till they die. At the mouth of two witnesses, or three witnesses, shall he that is worthy of death be put to death; but at the mouth of one witness, he shall not be put to death. The hands of the witnesses shall be first upon him to put him to death, and afterward the hands of all the people. So thou shalt put the evil away from among you."

1. The <u>SITUATION</u> involved – *"transgressing His covenant"*

2. The <u>SERVING</u> of other gods – v. 3 – *"served other gods, and worshipped them"*

3. The <u>STUDY</u> of the matter – v. 4 – *"inquired diligently"*

4. The <u>STONING</u> of the guilty – vv. 5-7

    (1) The <u>REQUIREMENT</u> of two or three witnesses

Matthew 18:15-20 – *"Moreover, if thy brother shall trespass against thee, go and tell him his fault between thee and him alone; if he shall hear thee, thou hast gained* *thy brother. But if he will not hear thee, then take with thee one or two more, that in the mouth of two or three witnesses every word may be established. And if he shall neglect to hear them, tell it unto the church; but if he neglect to hear the church, let him be unto thee as an heathen man and a tax collector. Verily I say unto you, Whatsoever ye shall bind on earth shall be bound in heaven; and whatsoever ye shall loose on earth shall be loosed in heaven. Again I say unto you that if two of you shall agree on earth as touching any thing that they shall ask, it shall be done for them by My Father, Who is in heaven. For where two or three are gathered together in My NAME, there am I in the midst of them."*

(2) The **RESPONSIBILITY**

of the witnesses – v. 7a

(3) The **RESULT** of such judgment – v. 7b – *"So thou shalt put the evil away from among you."*

BE **CAUTIOUS** IN BRINGING YOUR DISAGREEMENTS BEFORE THE PRIESTS AND/OR JUDGES – vv. 8-13

"If there arise a matter too hard for thee in judgment, between blood and blood, between plea ad plea, and between stroke and stroke, being matters of controversy within thy gates, then shalt thou arise, and get thee up into the place which the LORD

thy God shall choose; And thou shalt come unto the priests, the Levites, and unto the judge who shall be in those days, and inquire, and they shall show thee the sentence of judgment. And thou shalt do according to the sentence, which they of that place which the LORD shall choose shall show thee, and thou shalt observe to do according to all that they inform thee: According to the sentence of the law which they shall teach thee, and according to the judgment which they shall tell thee, thou shalt do; thou shalt not decline from the sentence which they shall show thee, to the right hand, nor to the left. And the man who will do presumptuously, and will not hearken unto the priest who standeth to minister there before the LORD thy God, or unto the judge, even that man shall die;

and thou shalt put away the evil from Israel. And all the people shall hear, and fear, and do no more presumptuously."

1. The <u>ARGUMENT</u> is too difficult to solve without help – v. 8

2. The <u>ANSWER</u> they give must be obeyed – vv. 9-11

3. The <u>ACCOUNTABILITY</u> brings serious consequences – vv. 12-13

    (1) <u>DEATH</u> to the one who rebels – v.12b

    (2) <u>DETERMINATION</u> by others to obey – v. 13

BE <u>CONCERNED</u> ABOUT THE DESIRE FOR A KING

LIKE ALL THE NATIONS AROUND YOU – vv. 14-20

"When thou art come unto the Land which the LORD thy God giveth thee, and shalt possess it, and shalt dwell therein, and shalt say, I will set a king over me, like all the nations that are about me; Thou shalt in any wise set him king over thee whom the LORD thy God shall choose: one from among thy brethren shalt thou set king over thee; thou mayest not set a stranger over thee, who is not thy brother. But he shall not multiply horses to himself, nor cause the people to return to Egypt, to the end that he should multiply horses; forasmuch as the LORD hath said unto you, Ye shall henceforth return no more that way. Neither shall he multiply wives to himself, that his heart

turn not away; neither shall he greatly multiply to himself silver and gold. And it shall be, when he sitteth upon the throne of his kingdom, that he shall write him a copy of this law in a book out of that which is before the priest, the Levites; And it shall be with him, and he shall read therein all the days of his life, that he may learn to fear the LORD his God, to keep all the words of this law and these statutes, to do them, That his heart be not lifted up above his brethren, and that he turn not aside from the commandment, to the right hand, or to the left; to the end that he may prolong his days in his kingdom, he, and his children, in the midst of Israel."

1. The <u>CHOICE</u> comes from the LORD – v. 15

2. The <u>CONDITIONS</u> that must be met – vv. 16-17

   (1) Don't multiply horses!

   (2) Don't multiply wives!

   (3) Don't multiply silver and gold – I Kings 10:27

3. The <u>COPY</u> of the law of God – vv. 18-20

   (1) His <u>RESPONSIBILITY</u> to that law of God

   (2) His <u>RESPONSE</u> to that law of God

   (3) The <u>REASON</u> behind this – v. 20

   To <u>ELIMINATE</u> pride!

   To <u>EXHORT</u> himself to not trust

his own opinions or wisdom!

To **EXTEND** his rule!

The **COMING** of a prophet -
Deuteronomy 18:1-22

The **PROVISION** for the priests – 18:1-8

1. The **SURVIVAL** of the priest – vv. 1-2

"The Levitical priests, that is all the tribe of Levi, shall have no part nor inheritance with Israel; they shall eat the offerings of the LORD made by fire, and his inheritance. Therefor shall they

have no inheritance among their brethren; the LORD is their inheritance, as He hath said unto them."

    (1) Their **PART** in Israel's inheritance was not given to them.

    (2) The **PREEMINENCE** of the LORD in their lives – *"the LORD is their inheritance"*

2. The **SUPPLIES** for the priest – vv. 3-4

"And this shall be the priest's due from the people, from them who offer a sacrifice, whether it be ox or sheep; and they shall give unto the priest the shoulder, and the two cheeks, and the maw. The first fruit also of thy corn, or thy

wine, and of thine oil, and the first of the fleece of thy sheep, shalt thou give him."

3. The <u>SELECTION</u> of the priest – v. 5

"For the LORD thy God hath chosen him out of all thy tribes, to stand to minister in the NAME of the LORD, him and his sons forever."

4. The <u>SERVICE</u> of the priest – vv. 6-8

"And if a Levite come from any of thy gates out of all Israel, where he sojourned, and come with all the desire of his mind unto the place which the LORD shall choose, Then he shall minister in the NAME of the LORD his God, as all his brethren the Levites do, who stand before the LORD. They shall have like portions to eat,

beside that which cometh of the sale of his patrimony."

The <u>PRACTICES</u> that must be avoided – vv. 9-14

1. The <u>LEARNING</u> of pagan practices must be avoided – v. 9 – *"thou shalt not learn to do after the abominations of those nations"*

2. The <u>LISTING</u> of such occultic and pagan practices – vv. 10-11

    (1) <u>SACRIFICING</u> your children

    (2) <u>SEEKING</u> information from demonic sources

3. The <u>LESSON</u> of the LORD God – vv. 12-14 – *"Thou shalt be perfect with the LORD thy God"*

The **PROPHET** whom God will raise up – vv. 15-22

1. Their **DUTY** to listen to him – v. 15 – *"unto him ye shall hearken"*

2. Their **DESIRE** to have someone like Moses – vv. 16-17 – *"according to all that thou desiredst of the LORD thy God in Horeb…"*

3. His **DEPENDENCY** upon the command of the LORD – v. 18 *"he shall speak unto them all that I shall command him"*

4. The **DECISION** to obey is crucial – v. 19 – *"I will require it of him"*

5. The **DANGER** which the prophet will face if it is not the word of the LORD – v. 20

– *"even that prophet shall die"*

6. The **DIFFERENCE** can be known by the outcome of his words – vv. 21-22 – *"if the things follow not, nor come to pass, that is the thing which the LORD hath not spoken."*

The **CITIES** of judgment –
Deuteronomy 19:1-21

The **CITIES** to which people can flee – vv. 1-3

"When the LORD thy God hath cut off the nations, whose Land the LORD thy God giveth thee, and thou succeedest them, and dwellest in their cities, and in their houses, Thou shalt separate three cities for thee in the midst of thy Land, which the LORD thy God giveth thee to possess. Thou shalt prepare thee a way, and divide the coasts of thy Land, which the LORD thy God giveth thee to inherit, into three parts, that every slayer may flee there."

1. When the LORD **DESTROYS** the nations – v. 1a

2. When Israel **DWELLS** in them – v. 1b

3. When the LORD **DISTRIBUTES** the Land – v. 2

4. When Israel **DIVIDES** the Land – v. 3

The **CASE** for which the cities are selected – vv. 4-10

1. The **REASON** involved – v. 4a *"that he may live"*

2. The **REALIZATION** of motive – v. 4b – *"Whoso killeth his neighbor ignorantly, whom he hated not in time past"*

3. The **RESULT** that occurred – v. 5 – *"the head (iron) slippeth from the helve (handle) and lighteth*

(striketh) upon his neighbor that he die"

4. The **REACTION** of the avenger – v. 6a – *"while his heart is hot"*

5. The **RESPONSE** to the LORD's commands – vv. 7-10 – *"then shalt thou add three cities more"*

    (1) Based on the **LOVE** you have for the LORD your God – *"to love the LORD thy God"*

    (2) Based on the **LIFESTYLE** which you have – *"to walk ever in His ways"*

    (3) Based on the **LESSON** you embrace – *"that innocent blood be*

not shed in thy Land"

The <u>CONSEQUENCE</u> for the one who commits murder – vv. 11-13

1. The <u>MOTIVE</u> is the crucial issue – v. 11a – *"But if any man hate his neighbor…"*

2. The <u>MURDER</u> is to be avenged – vv. 11b-12 – *"deliver him into the hand of the avenger of blood, that he may die"*

Genesis 9:6 – *"Whoso sheddeth man's blood, by man shall his blood be shed; for in the image of God made he man."*

Romans 13:3-5 – *"For rulers are not a terror to good works, but to the evil. Wilt thou, then, not be afraid of the power? Do that* *which is good, and thou shalt have praise of the same; For he is the minister of God to thee for good. But if thou do that which is evil, be afraid; for he beareth not the sword in vain; for he is the minister of God, a revenger to execute wrath upon him that doeth evil. Wherefore, ye must needs be subject, not only for wrath but also for conscience sake."*

   3. The <u>MANNER</u> in which the "elders" should respond – v. 13 – *"Thine eyes shall not pity him"*

The <u>COMMITMENT</u> to the landmarks that are established – v. 14

"Thou shalt not remove they neighbor's landmark"

The <u>CALL</u> for witnesses – vv. 15-21

1. **As to the <u>NUMBER</u> needed – v. 15 – *"one witness shall not rise up against man for any iniquity or for any sin"***

Matthew 18:15-20 – *"Moreover, if thy brother shall trespass against thee, go and tell him his fault between thee and him alone; if he shall hear thee, thou hast gained thy brother. But if he will not hear thee, then take with thee one or two more, that in the mouth of two or three witnesses every word may be established. And if he shall neglect to hear them, tell it unto the church; but if he neglect to hear the church, let him be unto thee as an heathen man and a publican. Verily I say unto you, whatsoever ye shall bind on earth shall be bound in heaven; and whatsoever ye shall loose on earth shall be loosed in heaven. Again I say unto you that if two of you shall agree on earth as touching any thing that they shall ask, it shall be done for them by My Father, Who is in heaven. For where two or three are gathered together in My NAME, there am I in the midst of them."*

    2. As to the <u>NEED</u> for careful investigation – v. 16

Exodus 20:16 – *"Thou shalt not bear false witness against thy neighbor."*

        (1)   The <u>PROBLEM</u> of a false witness – v. 16

        (2)   The <u>PERSONS</u> to judge – v. 17 – *"before the priests and the judges"*

(3) The **PUNISHMENT** that should be brought against the false witness – vv. 18-19a

(4) The **PURPOSE** behind this – v. 19b *"so that thou put the evil away from among you"*

(5) The **PRINCIPLE** of judgment – v. 21 – *"thine eye shall not pity; but life shall go for life, eye for eye, tooth for tooth, hand for hand, foot for foot."*

Matthew 5:38-42 – "Ye have heard that it hath been said, An eye for an eye, and a tooth for a tooth; But I say unto you that ye resist not evil, but whosoever shall smite thee on thy right cheek, turn to him the other also. And if any man will sue thee at the law, and take away thy coat, let him have thy cloak also. And whosoever shall compel thee to go a mile, go with him twain. Give to him that asketh thee, and from him that would borrow of thee turn not thou away."

The <u>CONFLICTS</u> that lead to war
Deuteronomy 20:1-20

The <u>PRESENCE</u> of the LORD is with them – v. 1
"for the LORD thy God is with thee"

Psalm 20:1-9 – *"The LORD hear thee in the day of trouble; the NAME of the God of Jacob defend thee; Send thee help from the sanctuary, and strengthen thee out of Zion; Remember all thy offerings, and accept thy burnt sacrifice. Grant thee according to thine own heart, and fulfill all thy counsel. We will rejoice in thy salvation, and in the NAME of our God we will set up our banners; the LORD fulfill all thy petitions. Now know I that the LORD saveth His anointed; He will hear him* *from His holy heaven with the saving strength of His right hand. Some trust in chariots, and some in horses, but we will remember the NAME of the LORD our God. they are brought down and fallen; but we are risen, and stand upright. Save, LORD, let the king hear us when we call."*

The <u>PRIEST</u> will encourage the people – vv. 2-4

"And it shall be, when ye are come nigh unto the battle, that the priest shall approach and speak unto the people, and shall say unto them, Hear, O Israel, ye approach this day unto battle against your enemies; let not your hearts faint, fear not, and do not tremble, neither be ye terrified because of them; For the LORD your God is He Who goeth with

you, to fight for you against your enemies, to save you."

1. Inward **COURAGE** – *"let not your hearts faint"*

2. Outward **CALM** – *"fear not, and do not tremble, neither be ye terrified because of them"*

3. Upward **CONFIDENCE** – *"For the LORD your God is He that goeth with you, to fight for you against your enemies, to save you"*

The **PROBLEMS** that might hinder them in battle – vv. 5-8

"And the officers shall speak unto the people, saying, What man is there who hath built a new house, and hath not dedicated it? Let him go and return to his house,

lest he did in the battle, and another man dedicate it. And what man is he who hath planted a vineyard, and hath not yet eaten of it? Let him also go and return unto his house, lest he die in the battle, and another man eat of it. And what man is there who hath betrothed a wife, and hath not taken her? Let him go and return unto his house, lest he die in the battle, and another man take her. And the officers shall speak further unto the people, and they shall say, What man is there who is fearful and fainthearted? Let him go and return unto his house, lest his brethren's heart faint as well as his heart."

1. A <u>HOUSE</u> that was not dedicated – v. 5

2. A <u>HUNGER</u> that was not satisfied – v. 6

3. A <u>HOPE</u> for a wife that was not realized – v. 7

NOTE: The word *"betrothed"* was normally done by paying the bride price (Hebrew: *mohar*) to the fiancée's father. Once the bride price is paid, the fiancée is considered legally married even though the wedding has not yet taken place.

4. A <u>HEART</u> that is not courageous – v. 8

The <u>PLACING</u> of captains over the people to lead them – v. 9

"And it shall be, when the officers have made an end of speaking unto the people, that they shall make captains of the armies to lead the people."

The **PEACE** that should be offered – vv. 10-11

"When thou comest nigh unto a city to fight against it, then proclaim peace unto it. And it shall be, if it make thee an answer of peace, and open unto thee, then it shall be that all the people who are found therein shall be tributaries unto thee, and they shall serve thee."

The **PUNISHMENT** upon those who will not make peace – vv. 12-18

"And if it will make no peace with thee, but will make war against thee, then thou shalt besiege it. And when the LORD thy God hath delivered it into thine hands, thou shalt smite every male thereof with the edge of the sword; But

the women, and the little ones, and the cattle, and all that is in the city, even all the spoil thereof, shalt thou take unto thyself; and thou shall eat the spoil of thine enemies, which the LORD thy God hath given thee. Thus shalt thou do unto all the cities which are very far off from thee, which are not of the cities of these nations. But of the cities of these people, which the LORD thy God doth give thee for an inheritance, thou shalt save alive nothing that breatheth, But thou shalt utterly destroy them, namely, the Hittites, and the Amorites, the Canaanites, and the Perizzites, the Hivites, and the Jebusites, as the LORD thy God hath commanded thee, that they teach you not to do after all their abominations, which they have done unto their gods; so should ye sin against the LORD your God."

1. The **EXHORTATION** to attack - v. 12

2. The **EXECUTION** of its male warriors – v. 13

3. The **EXCEPTIONS** that should be spared – vv. 14-15

4. The **EXTERMINATION** of those nations living within the inheritance Land which the LORD gave them – vv. 16-17

   THE PAGAN **CULTURES** – v. 17a

       HITTITES
       AMORITES
       CANAANITES
       PERIZZITES
       HIVITES
       JEBUSITES

THE CONTINUAL COMMAND OF THE LORD – v. 17B

THE DIVINE CAUSE BEHIND THIS INSTRUCTION – v. 18

The PRINCIPLE about the trees – vv. 19-20

"When thou shalt besiege a city a long time, in making war against it to take it, thou shalt not destroy the trees, thereof, by forcing an axe against them; for thou mayest eat of them, and thou shalt not cut them down (for the tree of the field is man's life) to employ them in the siege. Only the trees which thou knowest that they are not trees for meat, thou shalt destroy and cut them down; and thou shalt build bulwarks against the city that maketh war with thee, until it be subdued."

The **CONQUEST** of pagan cultures – Deuteronomy 21:1-23

The **DEATH** of a person when there is no evidence of how it happened or who did it – vv. 1-9

1. The **CITY** that is responsible for the investigation – vv. 1-3a

"If one be found slain in the Land which the LORD thy God giveth thee to possess, lying in the field, and it be not known who hath slain him, Then the elders and thy judges shall come forth, and they shall measure unto the cities which are found about him that is slain; And it shall be, that the city which is next unto the slain man..."

2. The <u>CUTTING OFF</u> of the heifer's head – vv. 3b-4

"even the elders of that city shall take an heifer, which hath not been wrought with, and which hath not drawn in the yoke; and the elders of that city shall bring down the heifer unto a rough valley, which is neither eared nor sown, and shall strike off the heifer's neck there in the valley."

3. The <u>COMING</u> of the priests – v. 5

"And the priests, the sons of Levi, shall come near; for them the LORD thy God hath chosen to minister unto Him, and to bless in the NAME of the LORD; and by their word shall every controversy and every stroke be tried."

(1) Their <u>ANOINTING</u> - *"to minister unto Him, and to bless in the NAME of the LORD"*

(2) Their <u>AUTHORITY</u> – *"by their word shall every controversy and every stroke be tried"*

4. The <u>CLEANSING</u> of the elders – vv. 6-8a

"And all the elders of that city, that are next unto the slain man, shall wash their hands over the heifer that is beheaded in the valley. And they shall answer and say, Our hands have not shed this blood, neither have our eyes seen it. Be merciful, O LORD, unto Thy people Israel, who Thou hast redeemed."

- (1) Their <u>CONFESSION</u> – *"our hands have not shed this blood, neither have our eyes seen it"*

- (2) Their <u>CRY</u> for mercy – *"Be merciful, O LORD, unto Thy people whom Thou hast redeemed"*

5. The <u>CONFIRMATION</u> of doing what is right – vv. 8b-9

"and lay not innocent blood unto Thy people of Israel's charge. And the blood shall be forgiven them. So shalt thou put away the guilt of innocent blood from among you; when thou shalt do that which is right in the sight of the LORD."

- (1) The <u>SYMBOL</u> of forgiveness – v. 8b

> *"and the blood shall be forgiven them"*

> (2) The <u>STANDARD</u> for handling it in this way – v. 9 – *"thou shalt do that which is right in the sight of the LORD*

The <u>DESIRE</u> for a woman taken captive – vv. 10-14

"When thou goest forth to war against thine enemies, and the LORD thy God hath delivered them into thine hands, and thou hast taken them captive, and seest among the captives a beautiful woman, and hast a desire for her, that thou wouldest have her as thy wife, Then thou shalt bring her home to thine house, and she shall shave her head, and pare her

nails, and she shall put the raiment of her captivity from off her, and shall remain in thine house and bewail her father and her mother a full month; and after that thou shalt go in unto her, and be her husband, and she shall be thy wife. And it shall be, if thou have no delight in her, then thou shalt let her go where she will. But thou shalt not sell her at all for money; thou shalt not make merchandise of her, because thou hast humbled her."

1. The **CIRCUMSTANCES** behind this – v. 10 – *"When thou goest forth to war against thine enemies, and the LORD thy God hath delivered them"*

2. The female **CAPTIVE** is desirable for marriage – v. 11 *"and seest among the*

captives a beautiful woman, and hast a desire unto her, that thou wouldest have her to thy wife'

3. The <u>CONCERNS</u> that must be handled carefully – vv. 12-13

    (1) The <u>HOUSE</u> where she will live

    (2) The <u>HEALTH</u> she will experience

    (3) The <u>HOME</u> she will miss

4. The <u>CULMINATION</u> of the marriage – v. 13b

5. The <u>CAUSE</u> for possible separation from her – v. 14

    (1) Don't <u>STOP</u> her from leaving!

    (2) Don't <u>SELL</u> her to make money!

The **DISTRIBUTION** of inheritance – vv. 15-17

"If a man have two wives, one beloved, and another hated, and they have borne him children, both the beloved and the hated, and if the firstborn son be hers that was hated; Then it shall be, when he maketh his sons to inherit that which he hath, that he may not make the son of the beloved firstborn before the son of the hated, which is indeed the firstborn. But he shall acknowledge the son of the hated for the firstborn, by giving him a double portion of all that he hath; for he is the beginning of his strength; the right of the firstborn is his."

1. The **PROBLEM** of having two wives

2. The <u>POSITION</u> of the firstborn is not dependent upon person feelings!

3. The <u>PORTION</u> of inheritance is to be greater for the firstborn – v. 17

The <u>DECISION</u> about a rebellious child – vv. 18-21

"If a man have a stubborn and rebellious son, who will not obey the voice of his father or the voice of his mother, and that, when they have chastened him, will not hearken unto them, Then shall his father and his mother lay hold on him, and bring him out unto the elders of his city, and unto the gate of his place. And they shall say unto the elders of his city, This, our son, is stubborn and rebellious. He will not obey our voice; he is a glutton, and a

drunkard. And all the men of his city shall stone him with stones, that he die. So shall thou put evil away from among you, and all Israel shall hear, and fear."

1. The <u>SITUATION</u> that exists – v. 18

    (1) <u>DISOBEDIENCE</u> to both parents

    (2) <u>DISCIPLINE</u> has not helped

2. The <u>SERIOUSNESS</u> of his rebellion is exposed – vv. 19-20 – *"a glutton, and a drunkard'*

3. The <u>STONING</u> of the son will affect many other families – v. 21

The <u>DEFILEMENT</u> that must be avoided in the case of one hanged on a tree – vv. 22-23

"And if a man have committed a sin worthy of death, and he be put to death, and thou hang him on a tree, his body shall not remain all night upon the tree, but thou shalt in any wise bury him that day (for he who is hanged is accursed by God), that the Land be not defiled, which the LORD thy God giveth thee for an inheritance."

1. The <u>CAUSE</u> for his death – *"committed a sin worthy of death"*

2. The <u>CURSE</u> that is to be removed by his burial – v. 22 *"for he that is hanged is accursed by God"*

The **CONCERNS** of relationships
Deuteronomy 22:1-30

The **CARE** of animals – vv. 1-4

"Thou shalt not see thy brother's ox or his sheep go astray, and hide thyself from them; thou shalt in any case bring them against unto thy brother. And if thy brother be not nigh unto thee, or if thou know him not, then thou shalt bring it unto thine own house, and it shall be with thee until thy brother seek after it, and thou shalt restore it to him again. In like manner shalt thou do with his ass; and so shalt thou do with his raiment; and with every lost thing of thy brother's which he hath lost and thou hast found,

shalt thou do likewise; thou mayest not hide thyself. Thou shalt not see thy brother's ass or his ox fall down by the way, and hide thyself from them; thou shalt surely help him to lift them up again."

1. The <u>LOST</u> shall be returned and restored – vv. 1-3

2. The <u>LIFTING</u> of those that fall – v. 4

The <u>CLOTHING</u> of male and female – v. 5

"The woman shall not wear that which pertaineth unto a man, neither shall a man put on a woman's garment; for all that do so are abomination unto the LORD thy God."

1. The <u>APPAREL</u> must be unique to your sexual gender!

2. The **ABOMINATION** unto the LORD thy God reveals that transsexuality is wrong!

The **CONCERN** for birds – vv. 6-7

"If a bird's nest chance to be before in the way in any tree, or on the ground, whether they are young ones, or eggs, and the dam sitting upon the young, or upon the eggs, thou shalt not take the dam with the young; But thou shalt in any wise let the dam go, and take the young to thee, that it may be well with thee, and that thou mayest prolong thy days."

1. **PROTECTION** of the mother – v. 6

2. **PROVISION** for the young – v. 7

The <u>CONSTRUCTION</u> of a house – v. 8

"When thou buildedst a new house, then thou shalt make a battlement for thy roof, that thou bring not blood upon thine house, if any man fall from there."

The <u>CO-MINGLING</u> that must be avoided – vv. 9-11

"Thou shalt not sow thy vineyard with divers seeds, lest the fruit of thy seed which thou hast sown, and the fruit of thy vineyard, be defiled. Thou shalt not plow with an ox and an ass together. Thou shalt not wear a garment of divers sorts, as of woolen and linen together."

1. When you <u>PLANT</u> seed – v. 9
2. When you <u>PLOW</u> with animals – v. 10

3. When you **PUT ON** a garment – v. 11

The **COVERING** with fringes – v. 12

"Thou shalt make thee fringes upon the four quarters of thy vesture, wherewith thou coverest thyself."

The word *"fringes"* is referring to "tassels" – the purpose to remember God's 613 commandments. The Hebrew word is *gedilim* which refers to the twisting of the braids.

The **COMMANDS** regarding sex and marriage – vv. 13-30

1. The **ACCUSATION** of a husband – vv. 13-14

"If any man take a wife, and go in unto her, and hate her, and give occasions of speech against her, and bring up an evil name upon her, and say, I took this woman, and when I came to her, I found her not a maid"

2. The <u>ACKNOWLEDGMENT</u> of the parents proving her virginity – vv. 15-17

"Then shall the father of the damsel, and her mother, take and bring forth the tokens of the damsel's virginity unto the elders of the city in the gate. And the damsel's father shall say unto the elders, I gave my daughter unto this man to wife, and he hateth her; and, lo, he hath given occasions of speech against her, saying, I found not thy daughter a maid. And yet these are the tokens of my daughter's virginity.

And they shall spread the cloth before the elders of the city."

   3. The <u>ACT</u> of the elders when the woman is not guilty – vv. 18-19

"And the elders of that city shall take that man and chastise him, And they shall amerce him in an hundred shekels of silver, and give them unto the father of the damsel, because he hath brought up an evil name upon a virgin of Israel; and shall be his wife; he may not put her away all his days."

    (1) <u>CHASTISEMENT</u> of the husband – v. 18

    (2) <u>COST</u> of 100 shekels to the wife's father – v. 19a

    (3) <u>COMMITMENT</u> to marriage without

any possibility of divorce – v. 19b

4. The <u>ACTION</u> taken if she is guilty – vv. 20-21

"But if this thing be true, and the tokens of virginity be not found for the damsel, then they shall bring out the damsel to the door of her father's house, and the men of her city shall stone her with stones that she die, because she hath wrought folly in Israel, to play the whore in her father's house; so shalt thou put evil away from among you."

5. The <u>ADULTERY</u> that results in death – v. 22

"If a man be found lying with a woman married to an husband, then they shall both of them die, both the man that lay with the

woman, and the woman. So shalt thou put away evil from Israel."

6. The <u>ABOMINATION</u> of immorality between an engaged woman and a man who is not her husband – in the city – vv. 23-24

"If a damsel who is a virgin be betrothed unto an husband, and a man find her in the city, and lie with her, Then ye shall bring them both out unto the gate of that city, and ye shall stone them with stones that they die; the damsel, because she cried not, being in the city; and the man, because he hath humbled his neighbor's wife. So thou shalt put away evil from among you."

7. The <u>ATTACK</u> when a man rapes an engaged woman in the field – vv. 25-27

"But if a man find a betrothed damsel in the field, and the man force her, and lie with her, then the man only that lay with her shall die. But unto the damsel thou shalt do nothing; there is in the damsel no sin worthy of death. For as when a man riseth against his neighbor, and slayeth him, even so is this matter; For he found her in the field, and the betrothed damsel cried, and there was none to save her."

8. The <u>ANSWER</u> when a man commits sexual immorality with a woman who is a virgin and not engaged – vv. 28-29

"If a man find a damsel who is a virgin, who is not betrothed, and lay hold on her, and lie with her, and they be found; Then the man who lay with her shall give unto the damsel's father fifty shekels of

silver, and she shall be his wife; because he hath humbled her, he may not put her away all his days."

9. The <u>ABUSE</u> of sex in the case of incest – v. 30

"A man shall not take his father's wife, nor discover his father's skirt."

The <u>CALL</u> and <u>CLEANSING</u> for worship –
Deuteronomy 23:1-25

The <u>CALL</u> to worship – 23:1-8

1. Physical <u>RESTRICTIONS</u> – v. 1

"He who is wounded in the stones, or hath his privy member cut off, shall not enter into the congregation of the LORD."

2. Immoral <u>RESTRICTIONS</u> – v. 2

"A bastard shall not enter into the congregation of the LORD; even to his tenth generation shall he not enter into the congregation of the LORD."

3. Ethnic **RESTRICTIONS** – vv. 3-6 – *"an Ammonite or Moabite shall not enter"*

   (1) The **EXTENT** of this restriction – *"forever"*

   (2) The **EXPLANATION** for this restriction

   They **PROVIDED** no bread and water – v. 4a

   They **PERSUADED** Balaam to curse Israel – v. 4b

   (3) The **EXPRESSION** of God's love for Israel – v. 5 – *"because the LORD thy God loved thee"*

   (4) The **EXHORTATION** about any future relationships – v. 6 – *"Thou shalt not seek their peace nor their*

prosperity all thy days forever."

The <u>CLEANSING</u> that is essential – vv. 9-14

"When the host goeth forth against thine enemies, then keep thee from every wicked thing. If there be among you any man who is not clean by reason of uncleanness that chanceth him by night, then shall he go abroad out of the camp; he shall not come within the camp. But it shall be, when evening cometh on, he shall wash himself with water and, when the sun is down, he shall come into the camp again. Thou shalt have a place also outside the camp where thou shalt go forth abroad. And thou shalt have a paddle upon the weapon; and it shall be, when thou wilt ease thyself abroad, thou shalt dig

therewith, and shalt turn back and cover that which cometh from thee. For the LORD thy God walketh in the midst of thy camp, to deliver thee, and to give up thine enemies before thee; therefore shall thy camp be holy, that He see no unclean thing in thee, and turn away from thee."

1. The **PRINCIPLE** involved – v. 9 - *"keep thee from every wicked thing"*

2. The **PERSON** that is unclean – vv. 10-11

3. The **PLACE** for excrement – vv. 12-13

4. The **PURPOSE** of the LORD behind all of this cleansing – v. 14 – *"therefore shall thy camp be holy"*

The <u>COMING</u> of another man's servant- vv. 15-16

"Thou shalt not deliver unto his master the servant who is escaped from his master unto thee; He shall dwell with thee, even among you, in that place which he shall choose in one of thy gates, where it liketh him best; thou shalt not oppress him."

1. No <u>SENDING</u> him back!

2. No <u>SUFFERING</u> on him!

The <u>CURSE</u> of immorality – vv. 17-18

"There shall be no whore of the daughters of Israel, nor a sodomite of the sons of Israel. Thou shalt not bring the hire of a whore, or the price of a dog, into the house of the LORD thy God for any vow; for even both these are

abomination unto the LORD thy God."

The <u>CHARGING</u> of interest – vv. 19-20

"Thou shalt not lend upon usury to thy brother; usury of money, usury of victuals, usury of anything that is lent upon usury. Unto a stranger thou mayest lend upon usury, but unto thy brother thou shalt not lend upon usury, that the LORD thy God may bless thee in all that thou settest thine hand to do in the land to which thou goest, to possess it."

The <u>COMMITMENT</u> of a vow – vv. 21-23

"When thou shalt vow a vow unto the LORD thy God, thou shalt not be slack to pay it; for the LORD thy God will surely require it of

thee, and it would be sin in thee. That which is gone out of thy lips thou shalt keep and perform, even a freewill offering, according as thou has vowed unto the LORD thy God, which thou hast promised with thy mouth."

The <u>CONSUMING</u> of a neighbor's food – vv. 24-25

"When thou comest into thy neighbor's vineyard, then thou mayest eat grapes to thy fill at thine own pleasure; but thou shalt not put any in thy vessel. When thou comest into the standing corn of thy neighbor, then thou mayest pluck the ears with thine hand; but thou shalt not move a sickle unto thy neighbor's standing corn."

The **CONSIDERATION** of marriage and money matters –
Deuteronomy 24:1-22

Marriage Matters – vv. 1-5

"When a man hath taken a wife, and married her, and it come to pass that she find no favor in his eyes, because he hath found some uncleanness in her; then let him write her a bill of divorcement, and give it in her hand, and send her out of his house. And when she is departed out of his house, she may go and be another man's wife. And if the latter husband hate her, and write her a bill of divorcement, and giveth it in her hand, and sendeth her out of his

house; or if the latter husband die, who took her to be his wife, Her former husband, who sent her away, may not take her again to be his wife, after that she is defiled; for that is abomination before the LORD. And thou shalt not cause the land to sin, which the LORD thy God giveth thee for an inheritance. When a man hath taken a new wife, he shall not go out to war, neither shall he be charged with any business, but he shall be free at home one year, and shall cheer up his wife whom he hath taken."

1. The <u>DISCOVERY</u> of uncleanness – v. 1

The Hebrew words *"ervat davar"* – also used in Deuteronomy 23:14 and Matthew 19:3-12

The word *'ervat* means "nakedness" or "genitals" – School

of Shammai argued that it refers to sexual immorality. The problem with this view is that such a matter would be punished by death, not divorce!

    2. The <u>DEPARTURE</u> of a wife for remarriage – v. 2a – *"And when she is departed out of his house, she may go and be another man's wife"*

    3. The <u>DESIRE</u> to remarry the former wife is not permitted – v. 4 – *"she is defiled"*

    4. The <u>DECISION</u> to get married brings responsibilities upon the husband – v. 5

        (1)   The <u>PROBLEM</u> if he goes to war – *"he shall be free at home one year"*

        (2)   The <u>PURPOSE</u> for the delay – *"cheer*

up his wife which he hath taken"

MONEY MATTERS – 24:6-22

1. The <u>PLEDGE</u> shall not take away a man's means of livelihood or survival – v. 6

"No man shall take the nether or the upper millstone to pledge; for he taketh a man's life to pledge."

Exodus 22:26-27 – *"If thou at all take thy neighbor's raiment to pledge, thou shalt deliver it unto him by the time that the sun goeth down; For that is his covering only; it is his raiment for his skin: wherein shall he sleep? And it shall come to pass, when he crieth* *unto Me, that I will hear; for I am gracious."*

2. The <u>PUNISHMENT</u> for kidnapping and slavery – v. 7 – *"that thief shall die"*

3. The <u>PLAGUE</u> of leprosy must be handled carefully – vv. 8-9

"Take heed in the plague of leprosy, that thou observe diligently and do according to all that the priests, the Levites, shall teach you; as I commanded them, so ye shall observe to do. Remember what the LORD thy God did unto Miriam by the way, after ye were come forth out of Egypt."

Numbers 12;10 – *"And the cloud departed from off the tabernacle;*

and behold, Miriam became leprous, white as show: and Aaron looked upon Miriam, and, behold, she was leprous."

4. The <u>POOR</u> must be respected and honored – vv. 10-15

    (1)   Don't <u>STAND</u> in his house to receive a payment for what you have loaned to him – vv. 10-11

"When thou doest lend thy brother anything, thou shalt not go into his house to fetch his pledge. Thou shalt stand abroad, and the man to whom thou dost lend shall bring out the pledge abroad unto thee."

    (2)   Don't <u>SLEEP</u> with what he owes you if

it jeopardizes his manner of life - vv. 12-13

"And if the man be poor, thou shalt not sleep with his pledge. In any case thou shalt deliver him the pledge again when the sun goeth down, that he may sleep in his own raiment, and bless thee; and it shall be righteousness unto thee before the LORD thy God."

    (3)   Don't <u>SEND</u> him away without paying him each day – vv. 14-15

"Thou shalt not oppress an hired servant who is poor and needy, whether he be of thy brethren, or of thy strangers who are in thy Land within thy gates. At his day thou shalt give him his hire, neither shall the sun go down upon it; for he is poor, and sitteth

his heart upon it; lest he cry against thee unto the LORD, and it be sin unto thee."

5. The <u>PUNISHMENT</u> for sin is to be borne by the one who did it – v. 16

"The fathers shall not be put to death for the children, neither shall the children be put to death for the fathers; every man shall be put to death for his own sin."

6. The <u>PROCEDURES</u> that lead a person to remember the bondage of Egypt – vv. 17-22

"Thou shalt not pervert the judgment due the stranger, nor the fatherless, nor take a widow's raiment to pledge; But thou shalt remember that thou wast a

bondman in Egypt, and the LORD thy God redeemed thee from there; therefore I command thee to do this thing. When thou cutest down thine harvest in thy field, thou shalt not go again to fetch it; it shall be for the stranger, for the fatherless, and for the widow, that the LORD thy God may bless thee in all the work of thine hands. When thou beatest thine olive tree, thou shalt not go over the boughs again; it shall be for the stranger, for the fatherless, and for the widow. And thou shalt remember that thou wast a bondman in the land of Egypt; therefore I command thee to do this thing."

The **CONTROVERSIES** that must be resolved
Deuteronomy 25:1-19

1. The **EXERCISE** of legal punishment – vv. 1-3

"If there be a controversy between men, and they come into judgment, that the judges may judge them, then they shall justify the righteous, and condemn the wicked. And it shall be, if the wicked man be worthy to be beaten, that the judge shall cause him to lie down, and to beaten before his face, according to his fault, by a certain number. Forty stripes he may give him, and not exceed; lest, if he should exceed, and beat him above these with

many stripes, then the brother should seem vile unto thee."

    (1) The **RESPONSIBILITY** of the judges – v. 1 – *"they shall justify the righteous and condemn the wicked"*

    (2) The **RESULT** should be controlled – *"40 stripes – not exceed"*

2. The **ENCOURAGEMENT** of the ox when plowing – v. 4

"Thou shalt not muzzle the ox when he treadeth out the corn."

3. The **EXHORTATION** to care for a brother's family – vv. 5-10

"If brethren dwell together, and one of them die, and have no child, the wife of the dead shall not marry without the family unto a stranger; her husband's brother shall go in unto her, and take her to him as his wife, and perform the duty of an husband's brother unto her. And it shall be, that the first-born whom she beareth shall succeed in the name of his brother who is dead, that his name be not put out of Israel. And if the man like not to take his brother's wife, then let his brother's wife go up to the gate unto the elders, and say, My husband's brother refuseth to raise up unto his brother a name in Israel; he will not perform the duty of my husband's brother. Then the elders of his city shall call him, and speak unto him; and if he stand to it, and say, I like not

to take her, Then shall his brother's wife come unto him in the presence of the elders, and loose his shoe from off his foot, and spit in his face, and shall answer and say, So shall it be done unto that man who will not build up his brother's house. And his name shall be called in Israel, the house of him who hath his shoe loosed."

    (1)   The <u>**PERFORMANCE**</u> of a husband for the widow who has no child – v. 5

    (2)   The <u>**PRIORITY**</u> of the firstborn in taking his father's name – v. 6

    (3)   The <u>**PROBLEM**</u> when the brother

does not want to do it – vv. 7-8

(4) The **PROCEDURE** for the widow in presence of the elders – vv. 9-10

4. The **EXTENT** of a wife's involvement in defending her husband – vv. 11-12

"When men strive together one with another, and the wife of the one draweth near for to deliver her husband out of the hand of him who smiteth him, and putteth forth her hand, and taketh him by the secrets, Then thou shalt cut off her hand; thine eye shall not pity her."

5. The **EXCHANGE** of weights and measurements – vv. 13-16

"Thou shalt not have in thy bag divers weights, a great and a

small. Thou shalt not have in thine house divers measures, a great and a small. But thou shalt have a perfect and just weight; a perfect and just measure shalt thou have, that they days may be lengthened in the Land which the LORD thy God giveth thee. For all who do such things, and all who do unrighteously, are an abomination unto the LORD thy God."

    (1)   The <u>MOTIVE</u> is important – v. 15

    (2)   The <u>MANNER</u> in which God describes such deceit – v. 16

6. The <u>EXTERMINATION</u> of Amalek – vv. 17-19

"Remember what Amalek did unto thee by the way, when ye were

come forth out of Egypt; How he met thee by the way, and smote the hindmost of thee, even all that were feeble behind thee, when thou wast faint and weary; and he feared not God. Therefore it shall be, when the LORD thy God hath given thee rest from all thine enemies round about, in the Land which the LORD thy God giveth thee for an inheritance, to possess it, that thou shalt blot out the remembrance of Amalek from under heaven; thou shalt not forget it."

    (1)   <u>REMEMBER</u> what he did – vv. 17-18

    (2)   <u>REMOVE</u> him completely – v. 19

The **CARRYING** of the first fruits to God
Deuteronomy 26:1-19

The **TREASURE** of the Firstfruits – vv. 1-11

1. The **POSSESSION** of the Land when the firstfruits are gathered – vv. 1-2a

"And it shall be, when thou art come in unto the Land which the LORD thy God giveth thee for an inheritance, and possesses it, and dwelleth therein, That thou shalt take of the first of all the fruit of the earth, which thou shalt bring of thy Land that the LORD God giveth thee…"

2. The **PLACE** where the firstfruits should be brought – v. 2b – *"And shalt put it in a*

basket, and shalt go unto the place which the LORD thy God shall choose to place His NAME there."

3. The <u>PRIEST</u> is the one that receives the basket of firstfruits – vv. 3-4

"And thou shalt go unto the priest who shall be in those days, and say unto him, I profess this day unto the LORD thy God, that I am come unto the country which the LORD swore unto our fathers to give us. And the priest shall take the basket out of thine hand, and set it down before the altar of the LORD thy God."

Numbers 18:13 – *"And whatsoever is first ripe in the Land, which they shall bring unto the LORD, shall be thine; everyone that is clean in thine house shall eat of it."*

4. The **PROFESSION** that should be made unto the LORD God – vv. 5-10a

   (1) As to family **BACKGROUND** – v. 5

"And thou shalt speak and say before the LORD thy God, A Syrian ready to perish was my father, and he went down into Egypt and sojourned there with a few, and became there a nation, great, mighty, and populous."

   (2) As to severe **BONDAGE** – v. 6

"And the Egyptians evil entreated us, and afflicted us, and laid upon us hard bondage."

   (3) As to spiritual **BURDEN** – v. 7

"And when we cried unto the LORD God of our fathers, the

LORD heard our voice, and looked on our affliction, and our labor, and our oppression."

> **(4) As to physical <u>BRINGING</u> them into the promised Land – vv. 8-9**

"And the LORD brought us forth out of Egypt with a mighty hand, and with an outstretched arm, and with great terribleness, and with signs, and with wonders; And He hath brought us into this place, and hath given us this Land, even a Land that floweth with milk and honey."

> It was the <u>POWER</u> of the LORD that did it! v. 8

> It was the <u>PLACE</u> of God's great promise – v. 9

Exodus 3:8 – *"And I am come down to deliver them out of the hand of the Egyptians, and to bring them up out of that land unto a large and good Land, unto a Land flowing with milk and honey; unto the place of the Canaanites, and the Hittites, and the Amorites, and the Perizzites, and the Hivites and the Jebusites."*

Numbers 13:27 – *"And they told him, and said, We came unto the Land to which thou sentest us, and surely it floweth with milk and honey; and this is the fruit of it."*

Deuteronomy 1:25 – *"And they took of the fruit of the Land in their hands, and brought it down unto us, and brought us word again, and said, It is a good Land* *which the LORD our God doth give us."*

5. The **PRAISE** they should give to the LORD – vv. 10b-11

"And thou shalt set it before the LORD thy God, and worship before the LORD thy God. And thou shalt rejoice in every good thing which the LORD thy God hath given unto thee, and unto thine house, thou, and the Levite, and the stranger who is among you."

The **TITHING** that will bring the blessing of the LORD – vv. 12-15

"When thou hast made an end of tithing all the tithes of thine increase the third year, which is the year of tithing, and hast given it unto the Levite, the stranger,

the fatherless, and the widow, that they may eat within thy gates, and be filled, then thou shalt say before the LORD thy God, I have brought away the hallowed things out of mine house, and also have given them unto the Levite, and unto the stranger, to the fatherless, and to the widow, according to all Thy commandments which Thou hast commanded me. I have not transgressed Thy commandments, neither have I forgotten them. I have not eaten thereof in my mourning, neither have I taken away ought thereof for the dead, but I have hearkened to the voice of the LORD my God, and have done according to all that Thou has commanded me. Look down from Thy holy habitation, from heaven, and bless Thy people, Israel, and the

Land which Thou hast given us, as Thou didst swear unto our fathers, a Land that floweth with milk and honey."

1. The **IMPORTANCE** of the third year – v. 12 – *"the year of tithing"*

2. The **IMPACT** upon a person's obedience – vv. 13-14 – *"I have not transgressed Thy commandments, neither have I forgotten them"*

3. The **INVITATION** to the LORD for His blessing – v. 15 – *"Look down from Thy holy habitation, from heaven, and bless Thy people, Israel…"*

The **TEACHING** that will bring the blessing of the LORD to His people - vv. 16-19

"This day the LORD thy God hath commanded thee to do these statutes and judgments; thou shalt, therefore, keep and do them with all thine heart, and with all thy soul. Thou hast avouched the LORD this day to be thy God, and to walk in His ways, and to keep His statutes, and His commandments, and His judgments, and to hearken to His voice; And the LORD hath avouched thee this day to be His peculiar people, as he hath promised thee, and that thou shouldest keep all His commandments; And to make thee high above all nations whom He hath made, in praise, and in Name, and in honor, and that thou mayest be an holy people unto the LORD thy God, as He hath spoken."

1. **The need of inward <u>COMMITMENT</u> – v. 16 – *"keep and do them with all thine heart, and with all thy soul"***

2. **The need of outward <u>CONFORMITY</u> – v. 17 – *"to walk in His ways"***

3. **The need of upward <u>CONFIRMATION</u> – vv. 18-19 – *"as He hath promised thee"* and *"that thou mayest be an holy people."***

The <u>CURSES</u> to be remembered
Deuteronomy 27:1-26

The <u>STONES</u> of remembrance – 27:1-8

"And Moses, with the elders of Israel, commanded the people, saying, Keep all the commandments which I command you this day. And it shall be on the day when ye shall pass over the Jordan unto the Land which the LORD thy God giveth thee, that thou shalt set thee up great stones, and plaster them with plaster; And thou shalt write upon them all the words of this law, when thou art passed over, that thou mayest go in unto the Land which the LORD thy God giveth thee, a Land that floweth with milk and honey, as the LORD God

of thy fathers hath promised thee. Therefore, it shall be when ye are gone over the Jordan, that ye shall set up these stones, which I command you this day, in Mount Ebal, and thou shalt plaster them with plaster. And there shalt thou build an altar unto the LORD thy God, an altar of stones; thou shalt not lift up any iron tool upon them. Thou shalt build the altar of the LORD thy God of whole stones, and thou shalt offer burnt offerings thereon unto the LORD thy God. and thou shalt offer peace offerings, and shalt eat there, and rejoice before the LORD thy God. And thou shalt write upon the stones all the words of this law very plainly."

    1. The <u>MESSAGE</u> on these stones – v. 3 – *"write upon them all the words of this law"*

2. The **MOUNTAIN** where the stones would be placed – v. 4 – *"Mount Ebal"*

NOTE: Mount Ebal is just north of Shechem, and is the highest mountain in the area – over 3000 feet above sea level, but only 1200 feet above the valley where it stands.

3. The **MAKING** of these stones – vv. 5b-6a

   (1) The **PLASTER** – *"write upon the stones all the words of this law very plainly"*

   (2) The **PURPOSE** – v. 5 – *"there shalt thou build an altar unto the LORD thy God, an altar of stones."*

> To offer burnt offerings of total commitment – v. 6b
>
> To offer peace offerings of rejoicing – v. 7

> (3) The **PREPARATION** – v. 5b – *"thou shalt not lift up any iron tool upon them"*

The **SUMMARY** of Moses and the Levitical priests – vv. 9-13

"And Moses and the priest, the Levites, spoke unto all Israel, saying, Take heed, and hearken, O Israel: this day thou art become the people of the LORD thy God. Thou shalt, therefore, obey the voice of the LORD thy God, and do His commandments and His statutes, which I command thee

this day. And Moses charged the people the same day, saying, These shall stand upon Mount Gerizim to bless the people, when ye are come over the Jordan: Simeon, and Levi, and Judah, and Issachar, and Joseph, and Benjamin. And these shall stand upon Mount Ebal to curse: Reuben, Gad, and Asher, and Zebulun, Dan, and Naphtali."

1. The **PROCLAMATION** of their relationship to the LORD God – v. 9 – *"this day thou art become the people of the LORD thy God"*

2. The **PREREQUISITE** for that relationship – v. 10 – *"thou shalt therefore obey the voice of the LORD thy God to do His commandments"*

3. The <u>PRONOUNCEMENTS</u> of blessings and curses – vv. 11-13

   MOUNT GERIZIM – *"bless the people"* – **Simeon, Levi, Judah, Issachar, Joseph, and Benjamin**

   MOUNT EBAL – *"to curse"* – **Reuben, Gad, Asher, Zebulun, Dan, and Naphtali**

The <u>SHOUTING</u> of curses – vv. 14-26 – *"with a loud voice"*

At the end of each curse is the response of the people – *"And all the people shall answer and say, AMEN!"*

   1. <u>SECRET</u> sins – vv. 15-19

      (1)   IDOLATRY – v. 15

      (2)   MOCKING PARENTS – v. 16

- (3) MOVING PROPERTY LINES – v. 17
- (4) NO HELP FOR THE BLIND – v. 18
- (5) NO JUSTICE FOR THE NEEDY – v. 19

2. **SEXUAL** sins – vv. 20-23

- (1) INCEST with father's wife – v. 20
- (2) BESTIALITY – v. 21
- (3) INCEST with sisters – v. 22
- (4) INCEST with mother-in-law – v. 23

3. **SOCIAL** sins

- (1) UNPROVOKED VIOLENCE – v. 24

(2) MURDER OF THE INNOCENT – v. 25

(3) LACK OF VERBAL COMMITMENT TO GOD'S LAW – v. 26

The <u>CAUSES</u> of blessings and cursings – Deuteronomy 28:1-68

The <u>SECRETS</u> for great blessing – vv. 1-14

1. <u>PRODUCTIVITY</u> – vv. 1-6

"And it shall come to pass, if thou shalt hearken diligently unto the voice of the LORD thy God, to observe and to do all His commandments which I command thee this day, that the LORD thy God will set thee on high above all nations of the earth; and all these blessings shall come to thee, and overtake thee, if thou shalt hearken unto the voice of the LORD thy God. Blessed shalt thou be in the city, and blessed shalt thou be in the field. Blessed shall be the fruit of thy body, and the

fruit of thy ground, and the fruit of thy cattle, the increase of thy kine, and the flocks of thy sheep. Blessed shall be thy basket and thy store. Blessed shalt thou be when thou comest in, and blessed shalt thou be when thou goest out."

    2. <u>**POWER**</u> over your enemies – v. 7

"The LORD shall cause thine enemies who rise up against thee to be smitten before thy face; they shall come out against thee one way, and flee before thee seven ways."

    3. <u>**PEOPLE**</u> of God – vv. 8-10

"The LORD shall command the blessing upon thee in thy storehouses, and in all that thou settest thine hand unto; and He shall bless thee in the Land which

the LORD thy God giveth thee. The LORD shall establish thee an holy people unto Himself, as He hath sworn unto thee, if thou shalt keep the commandments of the LORD thy God, and walk in His ways. And all people of the earth shall see that thou art called by the Name of the LORD, and they shall be afraid of thee."

4. PLENTY of goods – vv. 11-12

"And the LORD shall make thee plenteous in goods, in the fruit of thy body, and in the fruit of thy cattle, and in the fruit of thy ground, in the Land which the LORD swore unto thy fathers to give thee. The LORD shall open unto thee His good treasure, the heaven to give the rain unto thy Land in its season, and to bless all the work of thine hand; and thou

shalt lend unto many nations, and thou shalt not borrow."

    5. <u>**PRINCES**</u> in the world – vv. 13-14

"And the LORD shall make thee the head, and not the tail; and thou shalt be above only, and thou shalt not be beneath, if thou hearken unto the commandments of the LORD thy God, which I command thee this day, to observe and to do them. And thou shalt not go aside from any of the words which I command thee this day, to the right hand or to the left, to go after other gods to serve them."

The <u>SORROWS</u> that disobedience will bring – vv. 15-44

1. **PRODUCTIVITY** will end – vv. 15-19

"But it shall come to pass, if thou wilt not hearken unto the voice of the LORD thy God, to observe to do all His commandments and His statutes which I command thee this day, that all these curses shall come upon thee, and overtake thee. Cursed shalt thou be in the city, and cursed shalt thou be in the field. Cursed shall be thy basket and thy store. Cursed shall be the fruit of thy body, and the fruit of thy land, the increase of thy kine, and the flocks of thy sheep. Cursed shalt thou be when thou comest in, and cursed shalt thou be when thou goest out."

2. **PERISHING** will come quickly – v .20 – *"The LORD shall send upon thee cursing, vexation, and rebuke, in all*

that thou settest thine hand to do, until thou be destroyed, and until thou perish quickly, because of the wickedness of thy doings, whereby thou hast forsaken Me."

3. <u>PESTILENCE</u> will cleave to them – vv. 21-22

"The LORD shall make the pestilence cleave unto thee, until He have consumed thee from off the land, to which thou goest to possess it. The LORD shall smite thee with a consumption, and with a fever, and with an inflammation, and with an extreme burning, and with the sword, and with blasting, and with mildew; and they shall pursue thee until thou perish."

4. **<u>PUNISHMENT</u> from God will come down upon them – vv. 23-29**

"And thy heaven that is over thy head shall be brass, and the earth that is under thee shall be iron. The LORD shall make the rain of thy land powder and dust; from heaven it shall come down upon thee, until thou be destroyed. The LORD shall cause thee to be smitten before thine enemies; thou shalt go out one way against them, and flee seven ways before them, and shalt be removed into all the kingdoms of the earth. And thy carcass shall be meat unto all fowls of the air, and unto the beasts of the earth, and no man shall fray them away. The LORD shall smite thee with madness, and blindness, and astonishment of heart; And thou shalt grope at noonday, as the blind grope in

darkness, and thou shalt not prosper in thy ways; and thou shalt be only oppressed and spoiled evermore, and no man shall save thee."

  (1) The <u>EARTH</u> will be as iron – vv. 23-24

  (2) Their <u>ENEMIES</u> will smite them – vv. 25-26

  (3) The <u>EVILS</u> of disease will strike them – vv. 27-29

5. <u>POSSESSIONS</u> will be lost – vv. 30-34

"Thou shalt betroth a wife, and another man shall lie with her; thou shalt build an house, and thou shalt not dwell therein; thou shalt plant a vineyard, and shalt not gather the grapes thereof. Thine ox shall be slain before

thine eyes, and thou shalt not eat thereof; thine ass shall be violently taken away from before thy face, and shall not be restored to thee; thy sheep shall be given unto thine enemies, and thou shalt have none to rescue them. Thy sons and thy daughters shall be given unto another people, and thine eyes shall look, and fail with longing for them all the day long; and there shall be no might in thine hand. The fruit of thy land, and all thy labors, shall a nation whom thou knowest not eat up, and thou shalt be only oppressed and crushed always; So that thou shalt be mad for the sight of thine eyes which thou shalt see."

6. <u>PEOPLE</u> will be captured – vv. 35-37

"The LORD shall smite thee in the knees, and in the legs, with a sore

botch that cannot be healed, from the sole of thy foot unto the top of thy head. The LORD shall bring thee, and thy king whom thou shalt set over thee, unto a nation whom neither thou nor thy fathers have known, and there shalt thou serve other gods, wood and stone. And thou shalt become an astonishment, a proverb, and a by-word among all nations to which the LORD shall lead thee."

7. **PROSPERITY** will be destroyed by insects – vv. 38-42

"Thou shalt carry much seed out into the field, and shalt gather but little in; for the locust shall consume it. Thou shalt plant vineyards, and dress them, but shalt neither drink of the wine, nor gather the grapes; for the worms shall eat them. Thou shalt

have olive trees throughout all thy coasts, but thou shalt not anoint thyself with the oil; for thine olive shall cast its fruit. Thou shalt beget sons and daughters, but thou shalt not enjoy them; for they shall go into captivity. All thy trees and fruit of thy land shall the locust consume."

8. **POPULARITY** will be reduced – vv. 43-44

"The stranger who is within thee shall get up above thee very high, and thou shalt come down very low. He shall lend to thee, and thou shalt not lend to him; he shall be the head, and thou shalt be the tail."

Their SUFFERING is the result of their sin and disobedience – vv. 45-47

"Moreover, all these curses shall come upon thee, and shall pursue thee, and overtake thee, till thou be destroyed, because thou hearkenedst not unto the voice of the LORD thy God, to keep His commandments and His statutes which He commanded thee; And they shall be upon thee for a sign and for a wonder, and upon thy seed forever. Because thou servedst not the LORD thy God with joyfulness, and with gladness of heart, for the abundance of all things."

The SERVING of their enemies – vv. 48-58

1. The SOURCE of these enemies – v. 48

"Therefore shalt thou serve thine enemies whom the LORD shall send against thee, in hunger, and

in thirst, and in nakedness, and in want of all things; and He shall put a yoke of iron upon thy neck, until He have destroyed thee."

   2. The <u>STRENGTH</u> of a particular nation – vv. 49-57

      (1)   The <u>DESCRIPTION</u> of that nation – vv. 49-52

"The LORD shall bring a nation against thee from far, from the end of the earth, as swift as the eagle flieth; a nation whose tongue thou shalt not understand; A nation of fierce countenance, who shall not regard the person of the old, nor show favor to the young. And he shall eat the fruit of thy cattle, and the fruit of the land, until thou be destroyed; who also shall not leave thee either corn, wine, or oil, or the increase of thy kine, or flocks of thy sheep, until he have destroyed thee. And

he shall besiege thee in all thy gates, until thy high and fenced walls come down, wherein thou trustedst, throughout all thy land; and he shall besiege thee in all thy gates throughout all thy land, which the LORD thy God hath given thee."

The **PLACE** from where they will come – *"from far"*

The **PROBLEM** they will create – *"a nation whose tongue thou shalt not understand"*

Their **PRESENCE** will be violent – *"a nation of fierce countenance"*

The **PRODUCE** of the land they will destroy – *"shall eat the fruit of thy* *cattle, and the fruit of thy land"*

(2) The <u>DEVASTATION</u> that will occur – vv. 53-57

"And thou shalt eat the fruit of thine own body, the flesh of thy sons and of thy daughters whom the LORD thy God hath given thee, in the siege, and in the straitness, wherewith thine enemies shall distress thee; So that the man who is tender among you, and very delicate, his eye shall be evil toward his brother, and toward the wife of his bosom, and toward the remnant of his children whom he shall leave; So that he will not give to any of them of the flesh of his children whom he shall eat, because he hath nothing left him in the siege, and in the straitness, wherewith thine enemies shall distress thee

in all thy gates. The tender and delicate woman among you, who would not adventure to set the sole of her foot upon the ground for delicateness and tenderness, her eye shall be evil toward the husband of her bosom, and toward her son, and toward her daughter, and toward her young one who cometh out from between her feet, and toward her children whom she shall bear; for she shall eat them for want of all things secretly in the siege and straitness, wherewith thine enemy shall distress thee in thy gates."

  (3) The <u>DANGER</u> that will happen if we do not obey the commandments of the LORD – vv. 58-62

"If thou wilt not observe to do all the words of this law that are

written in this book, that thou mayest fear this glorious and fearful Name, The LORD thy GOD, Then the LORD will make thy plagues wonderful, and the plagues of thy seed, even great plagues, and of long continuance, and sore sicknesses, and of long continuance. Moreover, He will bring upon thee all the diseases of Egypt, which thou wast afraid of, and they shall cleave unto thee. Also every sickness, and every plague, which is not written in the book of this law, them will the LORD bring upon thee, until thou be destroyed. And ye shall be left few in number, whereas ye were as the stars of heaven for multitude; because thou wouldest not obey the voice of the LORD thy God."

(4) The <u>DESTINY</u> that their disobedience would bring – vv. 63-68

"And it shall come to pass, that as the LORD rejoiced over you to do you good, and to multiply you, so the LORD will rejoice over you to destroy you, and to bring you to nought; and ye shall be plucked from off the land to which thou goest to possess it. And the LORD shall scatter thee among all people, from the one end of the earth even unto the other; and there thou shalt serve other gods, which neither thou nor thy fathers have known, even wood and stone. And among these nations shalt thou find no ease, neither shall the sole of thy foot have rest; but the LORD shall give thee there a trembling heart, and failing of eyes, and sorrow of mind. And thy life shall hang in

doubt before thee; and thou shalt fear day and night, and shalt have no assurance of thy life: In the morning thou shalt say, Would God it were evening! And at evening thou shalt say, Would God it were morning! For the fear of thine heart wherewith thou shalt fear, and for the sight of thine eyes which thou shalt see. And the LORD shall bring thee into Egypt again with ships, by the way whereof I spoke unto thee, Thou shalt see it no more again; and there ye shall be sold unto your enemies for bondmen and bondwomen, and no man shall buy you."

The **CONSEQUENCES** of blessings and curses
Deuteronomy 29:1-29

REMEMBER the words of the covenant – 29:1-9

1. The **PLACE** where they received the covenant (Moab and Horeb) – v. 1

"These are the words of the covenant, which the LORD commanded Moses to make with the children of Israel in the land of Moab, beside the covenant which He made with them in Horeb."

2. The **POWER** that the LORD displayed in Egypt – vv. 2-3

"And Moses called unto all Israel, and said unto them, Ye have seen all that the LORD did before your eyes in the land of Egypt unto

Pharaoh, and unto all his servants, and unto all his land. The great temptations which thine eyes have seen, the signs, and those great miracles."

Deuteronomy 4:33-39 – *"Did ever people hear the voice of God speaking out of the midst of the fire, as thou hast heard, and live? Or hath God assayed to go and take him a nation from the midst of another nation, by temptations, by signs, and by wonders, and by war, and by a mighty hand, and by a stretched out arm, and by great terrors, according to all that the LORD your God did for you in Egypt before your eyes? Unto thee it was shown, that thou mightest know that the LORD, He is God; there is none else beside Him. Out of heaven He made thee to hear His voice, that He might instruct thee; and upon earth He* *showed thee His great fire, and thou heardest His words out of the midst of the fire. And because He loved thy fathers, therefore He chose their seed after them, and brought thee out in His sight with His mighty power out of Egypt, To drive out nations from before thee greater and mightier than thou art, to bring thee in, to give thee their land for an inheritance, as it is this day. Know therefore this day, and consider it in thine heart, that the LORD, He is God in heaven above, and upon the earth beneath; there is none else."*

3. The **PROBLEM** which they experienced – v. 4

"Yet the LORD hath not given you an heart to perceive, and eyes to see, and ears to hear unto this day."

4. The **PROVISION** of the LORD during the wilderness – vv. 5-6 – *"I have led you 40 years in the wilderness"*

5. The **PURPOSE** of the LORD – *"that ye might know that I am the LORD your God"*

6. The **POSSESSION** of the land east of the Jordan River – vv. 7-8

7. The **PROMISE** of prosperity – v. 9 – *"that ye may prosper in all that ye do"*

REAFFIRM your commitment to God's covenant – vv. 10-21

1. They were **STANDING** in His presence – *"Ye stand this day all of you before the LORD your God."*

2. They were <u>STABLISHING</u> their relationship with the LORD – vv. 13-15

    (1) Its <u>AUTHORITY</u> – *"as He hath sworn unto thy fathers, to Abraham, to Isaac, and to Jacob"*

    (2) Its <u>APPLICATION</u> – *"him that standeth here with us…and with him that is not here with us this day* (future generations).*"*

3. They had <u>SEEN</u> the abominations of the Egyptians – vv. 16-17

<u>NOTE:</u> The words *"abominations"* and *"their idols"* are the Hebrew words *shikkutsim* and *gillulim* – they refer to detestable things like impure foods and excrement.

4. They had **STANDARDS** to prevent their turning away from the LORD – vv. 18-19 – *"bless himself in his heart"*

5. They were **SEPARATED** from God's people if they did not repent – vv. 20-21 – *"and the LORD shall blot out his name from under heaven"*

RECOGNIZE when judgment falls that the LORD had specific reasons – vv. 22-29

1. To **EXPOSE** the reasons that future generations will be able to see and understand – vv. 22-23

"So that the generation to come of your children who shall rise up after you, and the stranger who shall come from a far land, shall say, when they see the plagues of that land, and the sicknesses

which the LORD hath laid upon it, and that the whole land thereof is brimstone, and salt, and burning, that it is not sown, nor beareth, nor any grass growth therein, like the overthrow of Sodom and Gomorrah, Admah, and Zeboiim, which the LORD overthrew in His anger, and His wrath."

2. To <u>EXPLAIN</u> His anger to all nations – vv. 24-26

   (1) They <u>FORSOOK</u> the covenant – v. 25

   (2) They <u>FOLLOWED</u> other gods – v. 26

3. To <u>ESTABLISH</u> the seriousness of His covenant – vv. 27-28 – *"and the anger of the LORD was kindled against this Land, to bring upon it all the curses that are written in this book"*

4. To **EXHORT** them to obey that which was revealed to them – v. 29 – *"the secret things belong unto the LORD our God; but those things which are revealed belong unto us and to our children forever, that we may do all the words of this law."*

The <u>CALL</u> to repentance
Deuteronomy 30:1-20

Deuteronomy 30:1-10 is read in Jewish synagogues on the Sabbath preceding the Ten Days of Repentance (Rosh Hashanah to Yom Kippur).

1. It is a <u>PROMISE</u> of return — vv. 1-5

"And it shall come to pass, when all these things are come upon thee, the blessing and the curse, which I have set before thee, and thou shalt call them to mind among all the nations, to which the LORD thy God hath driven thee, and shalt return unto the LORD thy God, and shalt obey His voice according to all that I command thee this day, thou and

thy children, with all thine heart, and with all thy soul, that then the LORD thy God will turn thy captivity, and have compassion upon thee, and will return and gather thee from all the nations where the LORD thy God hath scattered thee. If any of thine be driven out unto the outmost parts of heaven, from there will the LORD thy God gather thee, and from there will He fetch thee. And the LORD thy God will bring thee into the Land which thy fathers possessed, and thou shalt possess it; and He will do thee good, and multiply thee above thy fathers."

2. It is a <u>PLEA</u> for inward repentance – v. 6 – *"the LORD thy God will circumcise thine heart, and the heart of thy seed, to love the LORD thy God with all*

thine heart, and with all thy soul.

3. It is a **PUNISHMENT** upon Israel's enemies – v. 7 – *"And the LORD thy God will put all these curses upon thine enemies, and on them who hate thee, who persecuted thee."*

4. It is a **PRODUCTIVITY** in the Land – vv. 8-9 – *"the LORD thy God will make thee plenteous in every work of thine hand...for the LORD will again rejoice over thee for good, as He rejoiced over thy fathers."*

5. It is a **PRIORITY** that must be a reality – v. 10 – *"if thou turn unto the LORD thy God with all thine heart, and with all the soul"*

<u>REALIZE</u> how close to you is God's commandment – vv. 11-14

    1. No need to <u>SEARCH</u> heaven or earth to find it – it is not hidden from thee – vv. 11-13

"For this commandment which I command thee this day, it is not hidden from thee, neither is it far off. It is not in heaven, that thou shouldest say, Who shall go up for us to heaven, and bring it unto us, that we may hear it, and do it? Neither is it beyond the sea, that thou shouldest say, Who shall go over the sea for us, and bring it unto us, that we may hear it, and do it?

    2. Our need is but to <u>SEEK</u> the LORD – v. 14 – *"But the word is very nigh unto thee, in thy*

mouth, and in thy heart, that thou mayest do it."

RESPOND to God by choosing life – vv. 15-20

1. The **CHOICE** is ours – v. 15 – *"See, I have set before thee"*

2. The **COMMAND** is clear – v. 16

 (1) To **LOVE** the LORD thy God!

 (2) To **WALK** in His ways!

 (3) To **KEEP** His commandments!

3. The **CONSEQUENCES** are severe – vv. 17-18

"But if thine heart turn away, so that thou wilt not hear, but shalt be drawn away, and worship other gods, and serve them, I

denounce unto you this day, that ye shall utterly perish, and that ye shall not prolong your days upon the Land, to which thou passest over the Jordan to go to possess it.

4. The **CHALLENGE** is obvious — vv. 19-20

    (1) **LOVE** the LORD!

    (2) **OBEY** what He says!

    (3) **CLEAVE** unto Him!

The <u>COURAGE</u> which Moses declared they would need
Deuteronomy 31:1-30

The <u>ENCOURAGEMENT</u> which Moses gave to the people – vv. 1-6

"And Moses went and spoke these words unto all Israel. And he said unto them, I am an hundred and twenty years old this day; I can no more go out and come in. Also the LORD hath said unto me, Thou shalt not go over this Jordan. The LORD thy God, He will go over before thee, and He will destroy these nations from before thee, and thou shalt possess them; and Joshua, he shall go over before thee, as the LORD hath said. And the LORD shall do unto them as

He did to Sihon and to Og, kings of the Amorites, and unto the land of them, whom He destroyed. And the LORD shall give them up before your face, that ye may do unto them according unto all the commandments which I have commanded you. Be strong, and of good courage, fear not, nor be afraid of them; for the LORD thy God, He it is Who doth go with thee; He will not fail thee, nor forsake thee."

1. As to his **PRESENCE** among them – vv. 1-2

    (1) His **AGE** – *"I am 120 years old"*

    (2) His **ABILITIES** – *"I can no more go out and come in"*

    (3) His **APPROVAL** - *"also the LORD

hath said unto me, Thou shalt not go over this Jordan"

2. As to the <u>POSSESSION</u> of enemy territory – vv. 3-5

    (1) The <u>DESTRUCTION</u> will come from the LORD!

    (2) The <u>DECISION</u> to replace Moses with Joshua!

    (3) The <u>DESIGN</u> behind these victories!

3. As to their <u>PERSUASION</u> – v. 6

    (1) Based on His <u>PRESENCE</u> – *"for the LORD thy God, He it is that doth go with thee"*

(2) Based on His **<u>PROMISE</u>** – *"He will not fail thee, nor forsake thee"*

The <u>EXHORTATION</u> that Moses gave to Joshua – vv. 7-8

"And Moses called unto Joshua, and said unto him in the sight of all Israel, Be strong and of good courage; for thou must go with this people unto the Land which the LORD hath sworn unto their fathers to give them, and thou shalt cause them to inherit it. And the LORD, He it is Who doth go before thee; He will be with thee; He will not fail thee, neither forsake thee; fear not, neither be dismayed."

1. As to <u>COURAGE</u> – *"Be strong and of a good courage"*

2. As to **COMPLETION** of the task – *"for thou must go with this people unto the Land which the LORD hath sworn unto their fathers to give them: and thou shalt cause them to inherit it."*

3. As to the **COMFORT** of God's presence – *"He it is that doth go before thee; He will be with thee, He will not fail thee, neither forsake thee: fear not, neither be dismayed."*

    (1) He **PREPARES** the way – *"go before thee"*

    (2) He **PLACES** Himself right beside you – *"He will be with thee"*

- (3) He <u>PROMISES</u> to keep His Word – *"He will not fail thee, neither forsake thee"*

- (4) He <u>PROCLAIMS</u> that there is no reason to be afraid – *"fear not, neither be dismayed"*

The <u>EXTENT</u> to which the people were to hear the word of the LORD – vv. 9-13

"And Moses wrote this law, and delivered it unto the priests, the sons of Levi, who bore the Ark of the Covenant of the LORD, and unto all the elders of Israel. And Moses commanded them, saying, At the end of every seven years, in the solemnity of the year of

release, in the feast of tabernacles, When all Israel is come to appear before the LORD thy God in the place which He shall choose, thou shalt read this law before all Israel in their hearing. Gather the people together, men, and women, and children, and thy stranger who is within thy gates, that they may hear, and that they may learn, and fear the LORD your God, and observe to do all the words of this law; And that their children, who have not known anything, may hear, and learn to fear the LORD your God, as long as ye live in the Land to which ye go over the Jordan to possess it."

1. The <u>RESPONSIBILITY</u> of the priests – *"At the end of every seven years, in the solemnity of the year of release, in the feast of tabernacles."*

2. The <u>READING</u> of the law – *"thou shalt read this law before all Israel in their hearing."*

3. The <u>REASONS</u> for this observance – *"that they may hear, and that they may learn, and fear the LORD your God, and observe to do all the words of this law."*

The <u>EXPOSURE</u> of the change in leadership – vv. 14-15

"And the LORD said unto Moses, Behold, thy days approach that thou must die. Call Joshua, and present yourselves in the tabernacle of the congregation, that I may give him a charge. And Moses and Joshua went, and presented themselves in the tabernacle of the congregation.

And the LORD appeared in the tabernacle in a pillar of cloud; and the pillar of the cloud stood over the door of the tabernacle."

1. The **CHARGE** to Joshua was needed – *"call Joshua, and present yourselves in the tabernacle of the congregation that I may give him a charge."*

2. The **CLOUD** of the LORD's presence and approval – *"and the LORD appeared in the tabernacle in a pillar of a cloud."*

The **EXPLANATION** behind the writing of a song – vv. 16-21

"And the LORD said unto Moses, Behold, thou shalt sleep with thy fathers; and this people will rise

up, and go a whoring, after the gods of the strangers of the Land, to which they go to be among them, and will forsake Me, and break My covenant which I have made with them. Then My anger shall be kindled against them in that day, and I will forsake them, and they shall be devoured, and many evils and troubles shall befall them, so that they will say in that day, Are not these evils come upon us because our God is not among us? And I will surely hide My face in that day for all the evils which they shall have wrought, in that they are turned unto other gods. Now, therefore, write this song for you, and teach it to the children of Israel; put it in their mouths, that this song may be a witness for me against the children of Israel. For what I shall have brought them into the

Land, which I swore to give unto their fathers, that floweth with milk and honey, and they shall have eaten and filled themselves, and waxen fat, then will they turn unto other gods, and serve them, and provoke Me, and break My covenant. And it shall come to pass, when many evils and troubles are befallen them, that this song shall testify against them as a witness; for it shall not be forgotten out of the mouths of their seed. For I know their imagination which they go about, even now before I have brought them into the Land which I swore to give them."

1. The <u>REASON</u> behind it – vv. 16-18 – *"this people will rise up, and go a-whoring after the gods of the strangers of the Land...and will forsake Me, and break My covenant*

which I have made with them."

2. The <u>RESPONSE</u> of the LORD – v. 17a – *"My anger shall be kindled against them in that day, and I will forsake them."*

3. The <u>RESPONSIBILITY</u> for Moses – vv. 19-21 – *"teach it to the children of Israel; put it in their mouths, that this song may be a witness for Me against the children of Israel."*

The <u>EXAMPLE</u> of rebellion which had characterized them – vv. 22-30

"Moses, therefore, wrote this song the same day, and taught; it to the children of Israel. And he gave Joshua, the son of Nun, a charge,

and said, Be strong and of good courage; for thou shalt bring the children of Israel into the Land which I swore to give unto them; and I will be with thee. And it came to pass, when Moses had made an end of writing the words of this law in a book, until they were finished, that Moses commanded the Levites, who bore the Ark of the Covenant of the LORD, saying, Take this book of the law, and put it in the side of the Ark of the Covenant of the LORD your God, that it may be there for a witness against thee. For I know thy rebellion, and thy stiff neck: behold, while I am yet alive with you this day, ye have been rebellious against the LORD; and how much more after my death! Gather unto me all the elders of your tribes, and your officers, that I may speak these words in their ears, and call heaven and earth to record against them. For I know that after my death ye will utterly corrupt yourselves, and turn aside from the way which I have commanded you, and evil will befall you in the latter days; because ye will do evil in the sight of the LORD, to provoke Him to anger through the work of your hands. And Moses spoke in the ears of all the congregation of Israel the words of this song, until they were ended."

1. The <u>PLACE</u> for the writing of the law – vv. 22-26 – *put it in the side of the Ark of the Covenant of the LORD your God"*

2. The <u>PATTERN</u> of rebellion – v. 27 – *"ye have been rebellious against the LORD"*

3. The **PURPOSE** behind the words of Moses – vv. 28-30 – *"For I know that after my death ye will utterly corrupt yourselves, and turn aside from the way which I have commanded you…"*

The **COMPLETION** of the Song of Moses and its dangers – Deuteronomy 32:1-52

It is the **MUSIC** that must be taught to God's people! (32:1-43)

1. It **RESPONDS** with worship – vv. 1-6

"Give ear, O ye heavens, and I will speak; and hear, O earth, the words of my mouth. My doctrine shall drop as the rain, my speech shall distill as the dew, as the small rain upon the tender herb, and as the showers upon the grass, Because I will publish the Name of the LORD; ascribe ye greatness unto our God. He is the Rock, His work is perfect; for all

His ways are judgment; a God of truth and without iniquity, just and right is He. They have corrupted themselves, their spot is not the spot of His children; they are a perverse and crooked generation. Do ye thus requite the LORD, O foolish people and unwise? Is not He thy father who hath bought thee? Hath He not made thee, and established thee?

    (1)   The <u>EXTENT</u> of it – "O ye heavens...and hear, O earth" – vv. 1-2

    (2)   The <u>EXALTATION</u> in it – "ascribe ye greatness unto our God" – vv. 3-4

    (3)   The <u>EXHORTATION</u> in it – vv. 5-6 – "O foolish people and

unwise...hath He not made thee, and established thee?"

2. It <u>REMEMBERS</u> how the LORD chose them — vv. 7-14

"Remember the days of old, consider the years of many generations. Ask thy Father, and He will show thee; thy elders, and they will tell thee. When the Most High divided to the nations their inheritance, when He separated the sons of Adam, He set the bounds of the people according to the number of the children of Israel. For the LORD's portion is His people; Jacob is the lot of His inheritance. He found him in a desert land, and in the waste, howling wilderness; He led him about, He instructed him, He kept

him as the apple of His eye. As an eagle stirreth up her nest, fluttereth over her young, spreadeth abroad her wings, taketh them, beareth them on her wings, So the LORD alone did lead him, and there was no strange god with him. He made him ride on the high places of the earth, that He might eat the increase of the fields; and He made him to suck honey out of the rock, and oil out of the flinty rock; Butter of kine, and milk of sheep, with fat of lambs, and rams of the breed of Bashan, and goats, with the fat of kidneys of wheat; and thou didst drink the pure blood of the grape.

(1) The <u>DIVIDING</u> of the nations from Adam – vv. 7-8

(2) The <u>DESCRIPTION</u> of His people – v. 9

— "the LORD's portion is His people, Jacob is the lot of His inheritance"

(3) The <u>DETAILS</u> of His care and provision for His people – vv. 10-14

His <u>EYE</u> was on them – *"apple of His eye"* – v. 10

The <u>EAGLE</u> was the illustration of His care – v. 11

Their <u>EATING</u> in the promised Land emphasized His abundant provision – vv. 12-14

3. It <u>REALIZES</u> what went wrong – vv. 15-18

"But Jeshurun waxed fat, and kicked. Thou art waxen fat, thou art grown thick, thou art covered with fatness; then he forsook God Who made him, and lightly esteemed the Rock of his salvation. They provoked Him to jealousy with strange gods, with abominations provoked they Him to anger. They sacrificed unto devils, not to God; to gods whom they knew not, to new gods who came newly up, whom your fathers feared not. Of the Rock Who begot thee thou art unmindful, and hast forgotten God Who formed thee."

    (1) Their <u>FATNESS</u> led them to forget Who provided for them – v. 15a

- (2) Their <u>FORSAKING</u> of God Himself was the result – v. 15b

- (3) They <u>FOLLOWED</u> other gods – vv. 16-17

- (4) They <u>FORGOT</u> The God Who made them – v. 18

4. It <u>REVIEWS</u> the response of God to their sin and disobedience – vv. 19-26

"And when the LORD saw it, He abhorred them, because of the provoking of His sons and His daughters, and He said, I will hide My face from them, I will see what their end shall be; for they are a very froward generation, children

in whom is no faith. They have moved Me to jealousy with that which is not God; they have provoked Me to anger with their vanities: and I will move them to jealousy with those who are not a people; I will provoke them to anger with a foolish nation. For a fire is kindled in Mine anger, and shall burn unto the lowest hell, and shall consume the earth with her increase, and set on fire the foundations of the mountains. I will heap mischiefs upon them; I will spend Mine arrows upon them. They shall be burnt with hunger, and devoured with burning heat and with bitter destruction; I will also send the teeth of beasts upon them, with the poison of serpents of the dust. The sword without, and terror within, shall destroy both the young man and the virgin, the suckling also with the man of gray hairs. I said, I would scatter them into corners, I would make the remembrance of them to cease from among men."

1. They **PROVOKED** Him – v. 19

2. They **PROVED** they had no faith in Him – v. 20

3. They **PRESENTED** Him with no choice but to punish them severely – vv. 21-26

    (1) The **ATTACK** of another nation – v. 21

    (2) The **ANGER** of the LORD – v. 22

    (3) The **ARROWS** of the LORD – v. 23

    (4) The **ANIMALS** of destruction – v. 24

(5) The <u>ANGUISH</u> of sword and terror – v. 25

(6) The <u>ABSENCE</u> of their national identity – v. 26

4. It <u>RECOGNIZES</u> God's mercy and judgment upon the nations!
vv. 27-35

"Were it not that I feared the wrath of the enemy, lest their adversaries should behave themselves strangely, and lest they should say, Our hand is high, and the LORD hath not done all this. For they are a nation void of counsel, neither is there any understanding in them. Oh, that they were wise, that they understood this, that they would consider their latter end! How

should one chase a thousand, and two put ten thousand to flight, except their Rock had sold them, and the LORD had shut them up? For their Rock is not as our Rock, even our enemies themselves being judges. For their vine is of the vine of Sodom, and of the fields of Gomorrah; their grapes are grapes of gall, their clusters are bitter. Their wine is the poison of dragons, and cruel venom of asps. Is not this laid up in store with Me, and sealed up among My treasures? To Me belongeth vengeance, and recompence; their foot shall slide in due time. For the day of their calamity is at hand, and the things that shall come upon them make haste."

1. His <u>CONCERN</u> about what they think – v. 27

2. Their <u>COUNSEL</u> was not wise – vv. 28-29

3. Their <u>CONFIDENCE</u> ignored the LORD – vv. 30-34

4. Their <u>CALAMITY</u> was at hand – v. 35

It <u>RELIES</u> upon God's intervention – vv. 36-43

"For the LORD shall judge His people, and repent Himself for His servants, when He seeth that their power is gone, and there is none shut up or left. And He shall say, Where are their gods, their rock in whom they trusted, which did eat the fat of their sacrifices, and drink the wine of their drink offerings? Let them rise up and help you, and be your protection. See now that I, even I, am He, and there is no god with Me: I kill, and I make alive; I wound, and I

heal; neither is there any that can deliver out of My hand. For I lift up My hand to heaven, and say, I live forever. If I whet My glittering sword, and Mine hand take hold on judgment,, I will render vengeance to Mine enemies, and will reward them who hate Me. I will make Mine arrows drunk with blood, and My sword shall devour flesh; and that with the blood of the slain and of the captives, from the beginning of revenges upon the enemy. Rejoice, O ye nations, with His people; for He will avenge the blood of His servants, and will render vengeance to His adversaries, and will be merciful unto His Land, and to His people."

1. Their <u>POWER</u> is gone because they trusted in the wrong thing – vv. 36-37

2. The **PROTECTION** of the LORD is what they need — vv. 38-39

3. The **PUNISHMENT** of God will come upon the nations who attack Israel — vv. 40-42

4. The **PLAN** of God is rooted in His mercy — v. 43

It is the **MESSAGE** to be taught to their children — vv. 44-47

"And Moses came and spoke all the words of this song in the ears of the people, he, and Hoshea, the son of Nun. And Moses made an end of speaking all these words to all Israel. And he said unto them, Set your hearts unto all the words which I testify among you this

day, which ye shall command your children to observe to do, all the words of this law. For it is not a vain thing for you, because it is your life; and through this thing ye shall prolong your days in the Land, to which ye go over the Jordan to possess it."

1. The <u>COMMITMENT</u> of their hearts is essential – v. 46a

2. The <u>COMMAND</u> to their children is necessary – v. 46b

3. The <u>CONSEQUENCE</u> of their obedience will affect their future in the Land – v. 47

It is the <u>METHOD</u> God used to conclude the ministry of Moses – vv. 48-52

"And the LORD spoke unto Moses that selfsame day, saying, Get

thee up into this mountain of Abarim, unto Mount Nebo, which is in the land of Moab that is over against Jericho, and behold the Land of Canaan, which I give unto the children of Israel for a possession; And die in the mount where thou goest up, and be gathered unto thy people, as Aaron, thy brother, died in Mount Hor, and was gathered unto his people; Because ye trespassed against Me among the children of Israel at the waters of Meribah of Kadesh, in the wilderness of Zin; because ye sanctified Me not in the midst of the children of Israel. Yet thou shalt see the Land before thee; but thou shalt not go there unto the Land which I give the children of Israel."

1. The **PLACE** where he was to go – vv. 48-50

2. The <u>PROBLEM</u> that was involved – v. 51

3. The <u>PROMISE</u> that would encourage him in spite of his disobedience – v. 53

The **COMING** of blessing upon the people –
Deuteronomy 33:1-29

The **SOURCE** of all blessing – vv. 1-5

"And this is the blessing, wherewith Moses, the man of God, blessed the children of Israel before his death. And he said, The LORD came from Sinai, and rose up from Seir unto them; He shined forth from Mount Paran, and He came with ten thousands of saints. From His right hand went a fiery law for them. Yea, He loved the people; all His saints are in Thy hand: and they sat down at Thy feet; every one shall receive Thy words. Moses commanded us a law, even the inheritance of the

congregation of Jacob. And He was King in Jeshurun, when the heads of the people and the tribes of Israel were gathered together."

1. The <u>MAN</u> God used – v. 1

2. The <u>MANIFESTATION</u> of God's power – v. 2

    (1) The <u>SHINING</u> of His power

    (2) The <u>SAINTS</u> that came with Him

    (3) The <u>SENDING</u> of His law - v. 2b

3. The <u>MOTIVATION</u> behind it – v. 3

4. The <u>MESSAGE</u> His people received – v. 4

5. The <u>MANNER</u> in which the blessing would be proclaimed

NOTE: The words *"he was king in Jeshurun"* would be difficult if it referred to Moses – that seems unlikely! These words should apply to God Himself for he is indeed the *"king in Jeshurun"*

Psalm 95:3 – *"For the LORD is a great God, and a great King above all gods."*

The SELECTION of the tribes for blessing – vv. 6-25

REUBEN – v. 6 – *"Let Reuben live, and not die; and let not his men be few."*

NOTE: Reuben's influence as the firstborn of Jacob's sons was greatly reduced because of his incestuous relationship with Bilhah (Genesis 49:3-4).

JUDAH – v. 7 – *"And this is the blessing of Judah: and he said, Hear, LORD, the voice of Judah, and bring him unto his people; let his hands be sufficient for him, and be thou an help to him from his enemies."*

LEVI – v. 8-11 – *"And of Levi he said, Let thy Thummim and thy Urim be with thy holy one, whom thou didst prove at Massah, and with whom thou didst strive at the waters of Meribah; Who said unto his father and to his mother, I have not seen him; neither did he acknowledge his brethren, nor knew his own children; for they have observed Thy word, and kept Thy covenant. They shall teach Jacob Thine judgments, and Israel Thy law; they shall put incense before Thee, and whole burnt sacrifice upon Thine altar. Bless, LORD, his substance, and* *accept the work of his hands; smite through the loins of them who rise against him, and of them who hate him, that they rise not again."*

NOTE: The Levites had no property, but were responsible for teaching and worship. They were also responsible for the *"Thummim"* and the *"Urim"* that were plates placed in a pouch on the priest's breastplate – it was a method of determining important decisions.

BENJAMIN – v, 12 – *"And of Benjamin he said, The beloved of the LORD shall dwell in safety by him; and the LORD shall cover him all the day long, and he shall dwell between his shoulders."*

NOTE: The reference to God dwelling *"between his shoulders"* might refer to God's protection and care as a parent who carried a small child on the back, that is *"between the shoulders."* Benjamin is promised a special place of safety and protection.

<u>JOSEPH</u> – vv. 13-17 – *"And of Joseph he said, Blessed of the LORD be his Land, for the precious things of heaven, for the dew, and for the deep that coucheth beneath, and for the precious fruits brought forth by the sun, and for the precious things put forth by the moon, and for the chief things of the ancient mountains, and for the precious things of the lasting hills, and for the precious things of the earth and fullness thereof, and for the good will of him who dwelt in the bush; let the blessing come upon the head of Joseph, and upon the top of the head of him who was separated from his brethren. His*

glory is like the firstling of his bullock, and his horns are like the horns of unicorns; with them he shall push the people together to the ends of the earth; and they are the ten thousands of Ephraim, and they are the thousands of Manasseh."

NOTE: The reference of Joseph's blessing from the LORD is detailed by the remark at the end of verse 17 – "they are the ten thousands of Ephraim, and they are the thousands of Manasseh."

Verse 16 speaks of the *"good will of Him that dwelt in the bush"* – no doubt a reference to Moses' experience with the burning bush – Exodus 3.

ZEBULUN and ISSACHAR – vv. 18-19

"And of Zebulun he said, Rejoice, Zebulun, in thy going out; and, Issachar, in thy tents. They shall call the people unto the mountain; there they shall offer sacrifices of righteousness, for they shall suck the abundance of the seas, and treasures hidden in the sand."

NOTE: **The reference to Zebulun** ***"going out"*** **probably indicates their maritime activities and fishing expeditions. Issachar's** ***"tents"*** **probably refers to his care of sheep.**

GAD – vv. 20-21 – *"And of Gad he said, Blessed be he who enlargeth Gad; he dwelleth like a lion, and teareth the arm with the crown of the head. And he provided the first part for himself, because there, in a portion of the lawgiver, was he seated; and he came with the heads of the people, he* *executed the justice of the LORD, and His judgments with Israel."*

NOTE: This is quite a contrast between Gad and Reuben – and illustrates that Gad became the prominent tribe east of the Jordan River.

DAN – v. 22

"And of Dan he said, Dan is a lion's whelp; he shall leap from Bashan."

This verse does not locate Dan in Bashan – in the Hebrew text it is the lion that leaps, not the tribe of Dan.

NAPHTALI – v. 23

"And of Naphtali he said, O Naphtali, satisfied with favor, and full with the blessing of the LORD, possess thou the west and the south."

According to Targum Jonathan, Naphtali's territory involved the Sea of Galilee – western and southern shores.

ASHER – vv. 24-25

"And of Asher he said, let Asher be blessed with children; let him be acceptable to his brethren, and let him dip his foot in oil. Thy shoes shall be iron and brass; and as thy days, so shall thy strength be."

The area that Asher possessed was known for its abundance of olive oil – a form of his name also means *"foot"* – a play on words.

The SECRET of the blessing of the LORD – vv. 26-29

"There is none like unto the God of Jeshurun, Who rideth upon the

heaven in thy help, and in His excellency on the sky. The eternal God is thy refuge, and underneath are the everlasting arms; and he shall thrust out the enemy from before thee, and shall say, Destroy them. Israel then shall dwell in safety alone; the fountain of Jacob shall be upon a land of corn and wine; also His heavens shall drop down dew. Happy art thou, O Israel! Who is like unto thee, O people saved by the LORD, the Shield of thy help, and who is the sword of thy excellence? And thine enemies shall be found liars unto thee, and thou shalt tread upon their high places."

1. **His exalted POSITION – v. 26 "none like unto the God of Jeshurun"**

2. **His continual PROTECTION – v. 27 – "the eternal God is thy**

Refuge, and underneath are the everlasting arms"

3. His abundant <u>PROSPERITY</u> – v. 28 – *"land of corn and wine"*

4. His blessed <u>PEOPLE</u> – v. 29 *"Happy, art thou, O Israel; who is like unto thee, O people saved by the LORD"*

The <u>CONCLUSION</u> of the life of Moses
Deuteronomy 34:1-12

The <u>PLACE</u> from which he saw the Land – vv. 1-4

"And Moses went up from the plains of Moab unto the mountain of Nebo, to the top of Pisgah, that is over against Jericho. And the LORD showed him all the Land of Gilead, unto Dan, and all Naphtali, and the Land of Ephraim, and Manasseh, and all the Land of Judah, unto the utmost sea, and the south, and the plain of the valley of Jericho, the city of palm trees, unto Zoar. And the LORD said unto him, This is the Land which I swore unto Abraham, unto Isaac, and unto Jacob, saying, I will give it unto

thy seed. I have caused thee to see it with thine eyes, but thou shalt not go over there."

1. It was a <u>REVELATION</u> from the LORD Himself – *"and the LORD showed him…"*

2. It was a <u>REMINDER</u> of God's promise – *"This is the Land which I swore unto Abraham, unto Isaac, and unto Jacob"*

3. It was a clear <u>RECOGNITION</u> of the people to whom God gave this Land – *"I will give it unto thy seed"*

4. It was a powerful <u>REALIZATION</u> of the importance of complete obedience to God – *"I have caused thee to see it with thine eyes, but thou shalt not go over thither."*

The **PECULARITY** of his death and burial – vv. 5-8

"So Moses, the servant of the LORD, died there in the land of Moab, according to the word of the LORD. And He buried him in a valley in the land of Moab, over against Beth-peor; but no man knoweth of his sepulcher unto this day. And Moses was an hundred and twenty years old when he died; his eye was not dim, nor his natural force abated. And the children of Israel wept for Moses in the plains of Moab thirty days. So the days of weeping and mourning for Moses were ended."

1. It was **PLANNED** by the LORD – *"according to the word of the LORD"*

2. He was **PUT** in a burial place that no one can find - *"no

man knoweth of his sepulcher unto this day"

3. He was **PERMITTED** to have unusual strength all his days – "120 years old…his eye was not dim, nor his natural force abated"

The **PEOPLE** mourned his death for 30 days – v. 8

"And the children of Israel wept for Moses in the plains of Moab thirty days. So the days of weeping and mourning for Moses were ended."

The **PERSON** who would replace Moses – v. 9

"And Joshua, the son of Nun, was full of the Spirit of wisdom; for Moses had laid his hands upon him. And the children of Israel

hearkened unto him, and did as the LORD commanded Moses."

The **PROPHET** of unusual blessing – vv. 10-12

"And there arose not a prophet since in Israel like unto Moses, whom the LORD knew face to face, in all the signs and the wonders which the LORD sent him to do in the land of Egypt to Pharaoh, and to all his servants, and to all his land, and in all that mighty hand, and in all the great terror which Moses showed in the sight of all Israel."

1. His **RELATIONSHIP** to the LORD – v. 10 – *"whom the LORD knew face to face"*

2. His **RESPONSIBILITY** in Egypt – vv. 11-12 – *"which the LORD sent him to do"*